THE
PLANT LOVER'S GUIDE
TO
SALVIAS

THE **PLANT LOVER'S GUIDE** TO
SALVIAS

JOHN WHITTLESEY

TIMBER PRESS
PORTLAND · LONDON

CONTENTS

55
150 Salvias for the Garden

189
Growing and Propagating

WHY I LOVE SALVIAS

Some people grow salvias for their showy flowers. Others grow them for their textured and often fragrant foliage.

I grow salvias not only for their intrinsic value as beautiful plants in a landscape, but also for the added wildlife they attract that enlivens my garden and my life. Planted strategically throughout my property, salvias create daily opportunities for me to observe hummingbirds, bees, and butterflies.

On summer and fall mornings, the droning buzz of hefty, glossy black carpenter bees greets me when I step out onto my deck at the break of dawn for my first sip of coffee. These bees begin their day early, drinking nectar from a container-grown *Salvia* 'Wendy's Wish'. It is barely light and I am only aware of the bees because of their urgent, persistent buzzing.

Later, when I step outside my front door to begin the day's work, a rigidly straight path of decomposed granite, confined by two-by-four edging, leads me from the front door to the gravel parking area where my truck awaits. Midway down the walk, a chest-high *Salvia clevelandii* (Cleveland sage) has eased itself into the path, leaning so that anyone walking there is gently encouraged to slow and step around. The placement of this particular salvia is perfect.

A glossy black male carpenter bee nectaring on the flowers of *Salvia clevelandii.*

The path from my front garden in late spring, with *Salvia clevelandii* leaning across the way.

I have started down this path many mornings to begin the day, only to pause and watch a hummingbird moving unhurriedly, sipping nectar from the tightly bunched whorls of blue flowers spaced along the slender woody stems, or to wait for the pipevine swallowtail butterfly, its blue-black coloring shimmering in the morning light, until it has flitted off after getting its fill of nectar. On days when there are no hummingbirds or butterflies to distract, I notice the loud buzzing of carpenter bees or bumblebees as they move hurriedly between flowers to gather pollen or nectar.

Even when not in flower, the Cleveland sage gives me reason to have planted it along a pathway. The stiff, gray-green leaves treat me and other passersby to a sharp, yet pleasant fragrance of crisp camphor overlaid with a blend of resinous desert scents—a fragrance that appeals to many, me included.

Across from the Cleveland sage, low-growing *Salvia lavandulifolia* (Spanish sage) puddles out over the wood edging onto the gravel path. For a month in midspring, this tidy plant with its narrow silvery gray foliage is topped by 8-inch (3-cm) spikes of large lavender-blue flowers. Nestled against the fine foliage of the intensely silver *Santolina*

Salvia greggii with fiery skipper.

Calm and observant, an Anna's hummingbird rests on a dried whorl of *Salvia clevelandii*.

chamaecyparissus (lavender cotton) with *Eriogonum umbellatum* (sulfur buckwheat) behind, this pleasing trio looks attractive year-round, whether in flower or not, a subtle blend of silver, gray, and light green.

The path I am following divides an area that is part meadow, part lawn. Edging this area is an informal hedge of *Salvia microphylla* 'San Carlos Festival', selected for this location because of its compact habit, substantive pebbled foliage, and short stems of colorful rose-red flowers. These cover the plants beginning in late spring, when the first flush of flowers opens, and continue sporadically through summer and fall. Behind this grouping is a lone plant of *S. heldreichiana* that has made a low mound of divided, gray-green leaves. The long, slender stems with deep lavender-blue flowers rise above the surrounding plantings, beckoning more pipevine swallowtails, bees, and hummingbirds.

Just before the path reaches the steps that lead down to the parking area, *Salvia spathacea* (hummingbird sage) has colonized in the partial shade cast by a nearby olive tree and is nestled up against silver-plumed *Miscanthus sinensis* 'Graziella'. The deep

Lavender-blue, low-growing *Salvia lavandulifolia* eases out into my front walk and interweaves with a neighboring santolina.

A pipevine swallowtail butterfly sips nectar from a large flower of *Salvia heldreichiana*.

olive green leaves of hummingbird sage are large and textured, forming a loose mat only a few inches high. In midspring the stout, vertical flowering stems rise up tightly packed with crimson-red flowers peeking through the dark calyces. Like Cleveland sage, hummingbird sage gives pedestrians reason to pause, as if waiting for the crosswalk light to change to green, until the hummingbird has finished its visitation.

These scenes that play out in the garden slow me down, stop me, make me aware of the active life in the garden, not unlike the ringing of a monastery bell as a reminder to be present. To grow salvias is to be awakened by all the senses. The hummingbird or the delicate flight of a butterfly brings me into the present, slowing me down on a morning when scattered thoughts are of the day ahead as I head to my truck. The sharp scent of Cleveland sage fills the air and the nose for an instant, just long enough to bring an awakened awareness to where I am—in that moment. These brief scenes encountered along a path of carefully chosen plants are why I garden, and why I plant salvias in my garden and in the gardens I design.

DESIGNING WITH FLOWERS, FRAGRANCE, AND FOLIAGE

Salvias mix well with roses to create a charming cottage garden combination.

Salvias provide a world of color, size, and texture for any garden style. Here *Salvia pratensis* adds a bright sweep of complementary purple to a colorful border at Mendocino Coast Botanical Gardens.

Designing with salvias opens a world of possibilities. Considering the wide diversity of plants in the genus *Salvia*, it is not difficult to find one or many salvias for any type of garden, in any climate zone. Their use in the landscape is as varied as the genus. Salvias are seen as groundcovers, as lively companions for roses, and as superb container plants. They are as comfortable in a formal perennial border as in a cottage garden setting, a formal herb garden, or a wildlife garden. Salvias can lend a lush tropical flavor or a lean, dry garden look. For every gardener and every gardening style, there is a multitude of salvias from which to choose.

This diversity of salvias includes annual bedding varieties as well as hardy, long blooming herbaceous and evergreen perennials for the coldest climates. In milder climates, salvias can be mainstays of the landscape, providing year-round interest of foliage, form, and flowers. A handful are perfectly adapted to the rugged regime of the rock garden, while several species from Asia are at home in the woodland garden, thriving in partial shade and mixing well with ferns, epimediums, and hellebores. For gardens in all zones, an array of salvias enlivens and brightens any setting by attracting the colorful energy of hummingbirds and other pollinators.

The perennial border entrance to the Los Angeles County Arboretum and Botanic Gardens in early summer is alive with robust sages including *Salvia clevelandii, S. leucantha,* and S. 'Indigo Spires' in full bloom.

Purple calyces remain after the lovely lavender-blue flowers of *Salvia africana-caerulea* fade.

The prominent chartreuse bracts of *Salvia mexicana* 'Limelight' contrast vividly with the intensely blue flowers.

A perfectly proportioned unfolding bud of the pink bract form of *Salvia wagneriana*.

The combination of blackish flowers, silver calyces, and green stems and leaves in *Salvia discolor* is superb.

Salvia Contributions
to the Landscape

The world of salvias offers many pleasures. It can be a riotous world with brilliant cacophonous displays of saturated color. It can be a quiet world of soft textures and flowers in blended pastels. Salvias in the garden can awaken us with the fragrance of their foliage and the sound of bees and hummingbirds at their flowers. It is a world that also invites close inspection to appreciate the artful beauty of buds unfolding and the varied shapes of their simple flowers.

Salvias have changed little since being introduced into gardens. They have maintained their wild beauty. There are no double-flowered salvias or mega-sized flowers on short, stocky plants. Few salvias are "new and improved." This is part of their charm. The same plant can be elegant and a bit unruly.

This wild simplicity makes salvias highly attractive to wildlife. Bees, butterflies, and hummingbirds often are constant companions to the flowers, which carry the plant's original intent—to attract pollinators. Overly hybridized plants can be selected for increased flower size, often losing the ability to produce nectar, which is what draws the insects and hummingbirds to the flowers. Salvias have not lost this key survival trait.

A wild mix of myriad salvias in bloom on the grounds of Flowers by the Sea in early fall.

The showy colorful bracts of *Salvia sclarea* last well after the plants are done blooming.

SHOWY FLOWERS

Salvias bring to gardens some of the most brilliantly colored flowers imaginable, from the truest blues to stunning reds, glowing oranges, hot pinks, richly vibrant purples, and pure whites. The colors are crisp, clean, and saturated. There are no redder reds or bluer blues to enliven our gardens.

Often the attractiveness of salvias results from the combination of the color of their flower petals and color of the calyx. This can provide either a striking contrast or a beautiful complement. The calyx is the part of the flower that functions as a protective cover, enclosing the unopened bud. When the flower opens and emerges, the calyx remains and often plays a prominent role in the color scheme of the plant. For instance, *Salvia mexicana* 'Limelight' has prominent chartreuse bracts that contrast vividly with its intensely blue flowers, and *S. leucantha* has soft purple sepals that create a lively contrast to its fuzzy white flowers. In the hybrid salvia 'Phyllis' Fancy' the combination is a subtle enhancement: the tubular flowers are white, flushed with pale lavender-pink, while the calyces are a rich lavender.

In some salvias, modified leaves or floral bracts become an integral part, or perhaps the dominant part, of the inflorescence. This is the case of the well-known and easily grown *Salvia sclarea* (clary sage). It also holds true for *S. viridis*, an annual often grown as a cut flower. While these are both very showy in the garden, their individual flowers are relatively insignificant.

Salvias for Cut Flowers

Salvia 'Costa Rican Blue'
Salvia heldreichiana
Salvia involucrata
Salvia leucantha
Salvia madrensis
Salvia sclarea
Salvia viridis

DRAMATIC FOLIAGE

Beyond the obvious visual appeal of the showy flowers, many salvias have foliage that contributes strong elements of color, texture, and fragrance to any landscape. The most textural salvias often have gray or silver foliage, such as *Salvia argentea* (silver sage). Many of the tropical species bring a bold, lush look to a landscape, with large, rich green leaves, often textured with prominent veins, pebbled surfaces, or a purple cast to the leaves.

Many salvias have fragrant foliage. This fragrance can range from florally sweet as in *Salvia elegans* (pineapple sage) to the sharp, acrid scent of *S. apiana* (white sage). Working among salvias is made more pleasant because of their scents. Pruning the twiggy *S. greggii* (autumn sage) can be tedious, but is certainly made more enjoyable by the gentle fragrance given off by bruising and trimming the fine foliage.

Salvia fragrances are varied, complex, and often difficult to describe. Rarely does one scent dominate to give a clearly describable fragrance. Ask someone to define the scent of *Salvia clevelandii*, and you will hear a range of descriptions. Gardener and writer-friend Joan Walters describes the scent of Cleveland sage as pungent with a touch of eucalyptus, mint, pine, musk, and earth, and compares it favorably to the invigorating fragrance after a rain in the desert. No wonder many gardeners are passionate about having Cleveland sage in their garden.

The fragrant, volatile oils in salvia leaves along with often sticky, resinous calyces are why deer rarely eat these plants. I garden in deer country and have installed gardens where deer are plentiful and watch from a discreet distance as I plant, waiting patiently until I finish to sample the plantings. After 4 or 5 months without rain, deer are desperate for greenery, yet they walk among the salvias rarely taking more than a nibble. I've watched nervously as a half dozen deer walked through my front garden, navigating between pots of various *Salvia greggii* hybrids in full flower waiting to be photographed, while only one young buck sampled a few flowers before moving on.

A few salvias have colorful or variegated leaves, which provide reason enough to grow the plants. Look at *Salvia officinalis* (garden sage), for example, the signature plant representing the genus *Salvia*. The foliage not only serves culinary purposes, it also provides color and texture in the garden.

Salvias with Dramatic Foliage

Salvia argentea

Salvia caudata
'El Cielo Blue'

Salvia daghestanica

Salvia elegans
'Golden Delicious'

Salvia hierosolymitana

Salvia koyamae

Salvia leucophylla

Salvia macrophylla
'Purple Leaf'

Salvia nana

Salvia nubicola

Salvia officinalis
'Icterina'

Salvia officinalis
'Purpurescens'

Salvia officinalis
'Tricolor'

Salvia sinaloensis

Salvia elegans 'Golden Delicious', a recent introduction seen here in the garden of Christy Santos, holds bright gold leaf color all season long.

Leaves of *Salvia officinalis* 'Purpurescens' are purple upon opening, turning green as they mature.

The colorful textured foliage of *Salvia sinaloensis*.

The furry, fuzzy basal leaves of *Salvia argentea* are a visual and textural delight calling out to be stroked.

The golden-edged leaves of *Salvia officinalis* 'Icterina' add interest to the ornamental garden and flavor in the kitchen.

Hardy Perennial Salvias

Many salvia species are hardy perennials, growing and blooming in spring and summer, dying back in fall or winter (winter dormant), and then reappearing the next year to repeat the cycle. Perennials bring a seasonal rhythm to the garden. A well-designed planting provides changing scenes of foliage and flowers from spring through fall, with winter being a traditional and welcome time of rest. Hardy perennial salvias bring strong color and form to the early summer border. They are perhaps best represented by the hybrids of *Salvia* ×*sylvestris* (woodland sage), particularly 'May Night', named Perennial Plant of the Year in 1997 by the Perennial Plant Association.

With their vertical, tightly packed flower spikes, these hardy salvias make classic, contrasting combinations with other perennials. A composition of blue-flowered salvias with golden yellow coreopsis, yellow or orange daylilies, or with the contrasting shape of flat-topped heads of yarrow is always pleasing. Graham Stuart Thomas in his timeless book *Perennial Garden Plants* recommends planting selections of *Salvia* ×*sylvestris* with oriental poppies or peonies.

Grasses and salvias make a pleasing pairing. Salvias have a natural wildness that complements the informal use of grasses. *Salvia verticillata* 'Purple Rain', with its dusky mauve-purple whorled flowers on often-arching

The intense concentration of purple flowers of *Salvia* ×*sylvestris* 'May Night' is set off by the rose 'Sally Holmes' and the silver foliage of a helichrysum behind.

Purple-flowered *Salvia recognita* and flat-topped yarrow complement each other in color and floral shape.

Salvia ×sylvestris Cultivars

THESE POPULAR PERENNIAL salvias are available in the nursery trade under a variety of names including *Salvia nemorosa* and *S. ×superba*. In this book I have chosen to list these collectively under *S. ×sylvestris*.

stems, is frequently seen in combination with strong vertical grasses or those with char-treuse foliage such as *Milium effusum* 'Aureum' (Bowles's golden grass). I have seen *S. azurea* combined with grasses in a number of gardens; its slender, unruly habit is right at home with cascading companions where its sky blue flowers can be splayed against the tawny stems of late-season grasses.

Salvia 'Bee's Bliss' weaving through a planting of deer grass in a garden in Stonyford, California.

SMALL DRY GARDENS

I opened this book with a walk through my own small front garden. This garden is located in a canyon of blue oak and grassland in northern California. The summers are hot, usu-ally reaching 90°F (32°C) daily from early summer through early autumn. Periods over 100°F (38°C) are common, and there are at least one or two periods during the summer when temperatures reach 105°–108°F (40°–42°C) for several consecutive days. Humid-ity is low and there is rarely any measureable rainfall for 4–5 months. While winter tem-peratures are relatively mild, the long, hot period without any precipitation makes it an extreme climate.

Many salvias excel under the rugged conditions of such a climate. Some of these species originate in California or the southwestern United States; others are native to the Mediter-ranean region or South Africa. The size of some plants makes them best suited for large gardens, while the scale of others matches much smaller gardens. Some of them will thrive

With its low-growing, compact habit, *Salvia* 'Flower Child' adds color in a contemporary-style garden without overwhelming the other plants.

in containers; others are best used as groundcovers where they can spread. What attracts gardeners to all of these salvias is their drought tolerance. Salvias are great plants for the dry garden. And yes, it is possible to have an attractive garden with minimal water use.

On suburban or city lots, where garden size is limited, the most desirable salvias have a tidy habit and blend easily with other drought-tolerant plants. Plenty of salvias meet these criteria. In fact, few other plants can claim as long a bloom season as many of these easy-to-grow salvias.

For adaptability, long season of bloom, and wide color choices, the selections of *Salvia greggii*, *S. microphylla*, and *S.* ×*jamensis* are indispensable. Flowering begins in mid-spring and continues well into the fall. The wiry, shrubby plants have small leaves, and their flowers are quite showy due to the broad lower lip. Several of these grow less than 2 feet (60 cm) tall such as 'Berzerkeley', 'Mesa Azure', and 'Ultra Violet'. Any of these hybrids could be planted singly to provide a spark of color or in mass to make a stronger statement. In general, the winter foliage is not strong in these salvias, so place them where winter interest is provided by other plants. Good pairings for this purpose might include grasses such as *Muhlenbergia dubia* (pine muhly), agaves with their strong structure, or evergreen shrubs such as the smaller rock roses—for example, *Cistus* 'Sunset' or *C. creticus* 'Lasithi'—the lavender *Lavandula* 'Goodwin Creek Grey', or a smaller rosemary such as *Rosmarinus officinalis* 'Mozart'.

A number of low-growing, small-leaved salvias are comfortable tucked in at the base of larger plants, growing between rocks, or easing over pathways. *Salvia chamaedryoides* (germander sage) provides a silver highlight along with its sky blue flowers. *Salvia lycioides* (canyon sage) has small green leaves and bright blue flowers. Good companions with these salvias include nepetas, germander, buckwheats, penstemons, yarrows, lavenders, California fuchsia, and grasses such as the smaller pennisetums, fescues, and helictotrichons. All of these plants require a sunny position, decent drainage, and a similar watering regime.

Salvia lavandulifolia in a dry garden.

Low drifts of gray in smaller dry garden settings could consist of the culinary sage, *Salvia officinalis*, or the cultivar 'Berggarten' with its bold, broad leaves. The related *S. lavandulifolia* spreads slowly, softening edges against rocks or pathways. These selections are evergreen and for a short period in late spring display a good show of blue flowers. Other possibilities include *S.* 'Nazareth', a probable selection of *S. officinalis*, with silver leaves, compact habit, and a sharp pungent, medicinal fragrance, and *S. pachyphylla*, which has more substantive, extremely fragrant silvery foliage and spectacular iridescent pink to purple inflorescences.

While some gardeners love the gray foliage associated with the Mediterranean garden style, others yearn to counter this ubiquitous silver and gray-green seen in many dry gardens. A handful of salvias, in addition to the previously mentioned hybrids of *Salvia greggii* and *S. microphylla*, while perhaps not exactly lush, can contribute some very satisfying shades of green. Among them, the South African *S. namaensis* (Nama sage) and its hybrid selection *S.* 'Savannah Blue' feature feathery, fresh green foliage that helps highlight silver-foliaged plants. The perennial *S. radula*, also South African, brings a strong upright element into the garden with its vertical spikes of showy white flowers. *Salvia* 'Sally Greenwood', a U.S. hybrid, is low growing and spreading with small, yet deep green

Salvia 'Mesa Azure' has a low habit, good foliage, and a long season of blue-purple flowers.

Salvia 'Sally Greenwood' used to good effect, softening the paving and stone wall with its bright green foliage.

Salvia greggii/microphylla Cultivars

A GREAT NUMBER of cultivars fall into this confusing complex of species, which includes *S. greggii*, *S. microphylla*, *S. ×jamensis* (naturally occurring hybrids between the first two species), *S. muelleri*, *S. coahuilensis*, and maybe others. Many nurseries have introduced cultivars from their own breeding programs with these species, and several series are available, including Ballet, Heatwave, Mesa, Stampede, Turbulent Sixties, and innumerable others named by hybridizers and gardeners around the world. In many cases, it cannot be determined under which species a given selection should be listed as the hybrids are now so interbred. Despite their imperfect naming, these shrubby salvias all have twiggy, woody stems and usually small fragrant leaves. They are all tough, durable plants that are drought tolerant but look better with occasional deep watering in summer. They come in an incredible assortment of flower colors and plant sizes. A sampling included in this book are *S.* 'Dyson's Joy', *S.* 'Flower Child', *S. greggii* 'Alba', *S. greggii* 'Variegata', *S.* Heatwave 'Blaze', *S.* 'Hot Lips', *S.* 'Javier', *S.* 'Mesa Azure', *S. microphylla* var. *neurepia*, *S. microphylla* 'San Carlos Festival', *S.* 'Raspberry Royale', *S.* 'Robin Middleton', and *S.* 'Tangerine Ballet'.

Vigorous growing and large, *Salvia* 'Hot Lips' forms a hedge at Navarro Vineyards in Philo, California.

Compact-growing *Salvia* 'Carl Nielson' planted among other low-growing, drought-tolerant plants—santolina, eriogonum, muhlenbergia, and penstemon.

The large shrubby form of *Salvia microphylla* var. *neurepia* in the Mendocino Coast Botanical Gardens.

Salvia sonomensis makes a beautiful groundcover at Tilden Regional Park Botanic Garden in Berkeley, California.

The large flower of *Romneya coulteri* (matilija poppy) contrasts beautifully with the blue whorls of *Salvia clevelandii* in Jeff Weir's garden in Sacramento, California.

Salvia 'Vicki Romo', a hybrid of *S. apiana* and *S. clevelandii*, in the morning light at Rancho Santa Ana Botanic Gardens.

A hybrid *Salvia pratensis* thrives in Denver Botanic Gardens with eriogonum, penstemon, and xeric perennials.

Top Salvias for Rock Gardens

PANAYOTI KELAIDIS, senior curator and director of outreach for the Denver Botanic Gardens and a plantsman of international renown, is passionate about all things horticultural, with a particular specialty in rock garden and alpine plants. Among the salvias he recommends for rock gardens are three species described in this book:

Salvia caespitosa
Salvia daghestanica
Salvia pisidica

leaves and quantities of purple-blue flowers on slender stems from spring through fall.

A place can (and should) always be found for a few of the California native sages in the small dryland garden. Smaller selections of the Cleveland sage, such as 'Winifred Gilman' or 'Pozo Blue', take little space bringing fragrant foliage and whorls of blue flowers—electric blue in the case of 'Winifred Gilman'. *Salvia* 'Carl Nielson', thought to be a hybrid between two California species, has leaves similar to the Cleveland sage but greener. *Salvia columbariae* (chia), with its stunning, deep blue flowers in whorls on single erect stems, is found on fast-draining gravel slopes and would thrive in fast-draining rock garden conditions.

AS GROUNDCOVER

In the spreading-out-and-across category of hardy perennial salvias, a number of species and hybrids are effective groundcovers and are often used to cover hard-to-handle slopes. *Salvia* 'Bee's Bliss' covers the ground with unbounded energy. Spreading easily 4 feet (1.2 m) across in its first season, even in marginal soils with limited water, it makes a sturdy choice to cover banks. One of its parent species, *S. sonomensis* (creeping sage), is tighter to the ground, but is equally vigorous though more temperamental in not liking summer water and winter wet. Locally, I find it growing in red clay soil on slopes or near pines that help absorb excess water with, of course, essentially no summer water.

The various selections and hybrids of *Salvia mellifera* (black sage) such as *S. mellifera* 'Terra Seca', *S.* 'Dara's Choice', or *S.* 'Mrs. Beard' are not only rugged, heat and drought tolerant, but also have long pollinator-attracting displays of blue flowers in late spring and early summer. Also effective for covering some ground but with more height is *S. leucophylla* 'Point Sal'. These tough, long-lived plants are attractive year-round.

I recall a planting of *Salvia leucophylla* 'Point Sal' in Red Bluff, California, a city which often has the honor of being the hottest spot in the north end of the famously hot Sacramento Valley. This planting was on an exposed slope, facing west, with no protection from the unrelenting afternoon heat. The shimmering reflective silver bank of the salvia above the Sacramento River on a hot summer afternoon made a strong statement in the landscape and also about its toughness and tenacity.

IN THE LARGE DRY GARDEN

In reaching out and up, perhaps the largest of the California native sages would be *Salvia* 'Desperado'. This hybrid of *S. apiana* (white sage) and *S. leucophylla* (purple sage) reaches 6–8 feet (1.8–2.4 m) tall and nearly as wide. Both *S.* 'Desperado' and the larger growing cultivars of *S. clevelandii*, which can reach 5 feet (1.5 m) tall, combine well with robust *Romneya coulteri* (matilija poppy). The poppy's bright green foliage and hand-sized, crepe papery white flowers with deep yellow centers make a striking counterpoint to the purple-blue whorls of these salvias. The white sage, when not in flower, is

Salvia glabrescens grows in a shady garden in the arid climate of Sparks, Nevada.

a compact plant, but when the 4-foot (1.2-m) wands of flowers erupt in all directions in early summer, it certainly takes up some room. This is not one to plant too close to a path.

Because the California and Mediterranean sages usually bloom from late spring to early summer, I look to the hybrids of *Salvia greggii* and *S. microphylla* to provide summer and fall color. While most of them are not considered large, a few do reach sizeable proportions. Select ones to fit the scale of the other plantings. For a large garden, placing them in groups makes more of an impact.

The bank below my house is planted with ceanothus, larger rock roses, and Jerusalem sage. Among these is a group of three plants of the large, vigorous *Salvia microphylla* var. *neurepia* placed against the butterfly rose, *Rosa mutabilis*. By planting three close together, the scale of the nearby plantings is maintained and the trio makes a bright spot of deep red for 9–10 months of the year. The hummingbirds and bees appreciate the long season of bloom. *Salvia* 'Hot Lips' would also have been a suitable choice.

IN THE COLDER DRYLAND GARDEN

In addition to the salvias that flourish in climates with long, hot, dry summers and mild winters, several thrive in areas of cold, dry winters and periodic monsoonal summer rainfall. In the United States, examples of this climate can be found in Colorado and parts of the Southwest, regions that fall in USDA hardiness Zones 5 and 6.

Denver Botanic Gardens (in Zone 5) and outlying municipal parks have perfected xeric borders and landscapes. By judiciously choosing native plants and plants from similar climates around the world, they have developed stunningly beautiful, long-blooming landscapes appropriate to their climate. A few of the perennial salvias that thrive in these conditions are *Salvia argentea*, *S. cyanescens*, *S. darcyi*, *S. recognita*, *S. ringens*, *S. sclarea*, *S. ×sylvestris*, *S. transsylvanica*, and some of the hardier forms of the *S. greggii/ S. microphylla* group.

The glowing flowers of *Salvia blepharophylla* 'Painted Lady' stand out in partial shade.

A premier plant for the rock garden, *Salvia daghestanica* forms low silvery gray mats and is adapted to very rugged conditions.

FOR THE WOODLAND GARDEN

A number of salvias are adapted to woodland conditions. Here partial shade from the tree canopy, humus-rich soil, and regular water combine to create the perfect situation. Salvias that grow in woodlands tend to have prominent clumps of large, deep green leaves, which in turn contrast nicely with finer-foliaged shade plants such as epimediums or ferns, or with variegated plants such as hostas or pulmonarias. Some of these woodland species, such as *Salvia koyamae* (Japanese yellow sage), spread slowly and over time make luxuriant groundcovers. While the flowers of woodland salvias can be spectacular with intricate markings, they rarely command attention. Instead, the delicate flowers complement the rich foliage of all the forest-dwelling plants. *Salvia amarissima*, *S. forsskaolii*, *S. glabrescens*, *S. nipponica*, *S. nubicola*, and *S. tomentosa* are other choice woodland salvias.

IN ALPINE AND ROCK GARDENS

Few, if any, salvias can be considered true alpine plants. For whatever reason, the well-traveled salvias have not evolved to grow in cold mountainous regions. However, several species from the mountains of Turkey are perfectly adapted to use in traditional rock garden settings. Most of these are mat-forming species with the typical Mediterranean silver-gray foliage. They require a spot in the garden with good drainage and full sun. Candidates for the rock garden described in this book include *Salvia caespitosa*, *S. columbariae*, *S. cyanescens*, *S. daghestanica*, *S. jurisicii* (feathered sage), *S. lycioides*, *S. muirii*, *S. pisidica*, and *S. thymoides* (thyme-leaved sage).

Red-flowered, tender *Salvia splendens* with annuals.

A blend of colorful tender salvias in early autumn includes (from front to back) *Salvia elegans* 'Frieda Dixon', *S.* 'Waverly', and *S. involucrata*.

Tender Salvias for Cold Climates

Unlike hardy perennial salvias, which reliably reappear in the garden after a cold winter, tender perennials do not. They require a tropical or subtropical climate to stay alive in winter. Nevertheless, gardeners in cold climates who want to grow tender salvias outdoors can do so by treating them as annuals.

I remember the days when I operated my mail-order nursery in sunny California and we would ship quantities of salvias all over the United States, including the East Coast, Midwest, and New England. Most were tender salvias that without some effort clearly would not survive winters in the places they were going. Adventurous gardeners were experimenting with these plants, using them as seasonal additions to their gardens.

The salvias would ship out from late spring to early summer depending on the destination climate. There they would be planted as soon as danger from frost was past and before summer heat set in. This gave the salvias a chance to make sizeable plants by midsummer, when they would often begin to flower. Year after year the same customers would order a half dozen each of *Salvia guaranitica* (anise-scented sage), *S. involucrata*, *S. leucantha*, *S.* 'Waverly', and others. These gardeners not only wanted the display of flowers from late summer through fall, but they were also looking to attract hummingbirds into their gardens.

This approach struck me then, as it does now, as an excellent way to bring a wide range of salvias into a garden. For gardeners wanting to expand their choices, my advice is to think impermanence. Think big annuals. Be willing to experiment, and be willing to let plants go at the end of the season.

A great plant to illustrate this approach is *Salvia* 'Indigo Spires', which, though perennial to Zone 8 (barely), has been used for many years as a large floriferous annual in colder zones. It grows 4–5 feet (1.2–1.5 m) tall, quickly sending out its unruly wands of blue-purple flowers for 3–4 months until the first solid freeze. The fact that it will need replacing next spring is a minor consideration for the length of its bloom and the wildlife it attracts to the garden. It earns its keep for the season.

FOR SEASONAL COLOR

There are many tender salvias to use as large annual highlights. The many tropical salvias from Mexico, Central and South America work especially well as they grow quickly and bloom in late summer and fall, qualities that make these species ideal for placing in an opening among shrubs, between roses, or in perennial gardens.

The colorful flowers of *Salvia curviflora* bloom from summer through fall.

In milder climates, there is less chance of losing tender salvias during the winter, thereby replacing them each year may not be necessary. But, even if prayers for a mild winter are not answered and that one cold spell is too much for the salvias, the plants will have provided much pleasure in your garden. Because so many of the salvias are tender, you can help relieve your worry and stress, and greatly expand your plant choices if you accept the enjoyment salvias bring during the summer and fall, and let them go at season's end.

One key to success in using salvias as seasonal color is to select plants that do not bloom too late for your climate. As previously mentioned, some of the tropical species bloom from late summer through fall, but others may not begin blooming until mid or late autumn. These late-blooming salvias are more of a gamble if you garden in a northern zone where hard frosts can come early.

Ignoring the hardiness factor and not worrying about whether a plant survives the winter opens the door to experimenting by bringing in some dramatic and colorful plants for the season. *Salvia* 'Amistad', a new hybrid from Argentina that became available in U.S. nurseries in 2013, is an excellent choice for adding deep purple flowers into the garden. It grows quickly to 4 feet (1.2 m) tall, flowering all summer and fall. Two other purple-flowered selections—'Purple Majesty' and 'Betsy's Purple'—tend to bloom later and in one season don't produce a high ratio of flowers to foliage as 'Amistad' does. This is a particularly floriferous and compact selection.

Few plants do purple as well as salvias, and the same is true with blue. Whether navy blue, sky blue, cobalt, or indigo, salvias certainly cover the blue spectrum. By planting any of the *Salvia guaranitica* selections, you are guaranteed true blue in the garden for

The desirable *Salvia* 'Amistad' has elegant purple flowers and rich green foliage on a compact plant.

A cheerful seasonal planting of *Bidens ferulifolia* with a cultivar of the tender *Salvia farinacea*.

A male Anna's hummingbird enjoys the flowers of a *Salvia involucrata* hybrid.

Salvia guaranitica and cannas match well for a cool, tropical look in the garden.

Salvias for Containers

Salvia 'Amistad'
Salvia blepharophylla
Salvia buchananii
Salvia caudata 'El Cielo Blue'
Salvia chamaedryoides
Salvia chiapensis
Salvia confertiflora
Salvia corrugata
Salvia curviflora
Salvia daghestanica
Salvia discolor
Salvia fruticosa
Salvia greggii/microphylla cultivars
Salvia guaranitica 'Black and Blue'
Salvia macrophylla 'Purple Leaf'
Salvia madrensis 'Red Neck Girl'
Salvia muirii
Salvia 'Mystic Spires Blue'
Salvia nana
Salvia officinalis
Salvia sagittata

months. All of them are good, particularly 'Black and Blue' and 'Blue Ensign'. Blooming from midsummer through fall, these selections are among the best salvias to attract hummingbirds. Plant them with late summer-blooming perennials such as asters, rudbeckias, helianthus, or heliopsis, or plant them with cannas for a lush effect. *Salvia guaranitica* can be reasonably hardy (Zone 7), but is still worth growing if it fails winter's test. Other good blue salvias to consider for summer color are *S. cacaliifolia* (Guatemalan leaf sage), *S. sagittata*, and the varieties of *S. patens* (gentian sage). These all begin blooming in midsummer and continue until frost.

Two long-blooming salvias, both of which prefer some shade in a climate with hot summers, are the import from Australia, *Salvia* 'Wendy's Wish', and *S. chiapensis* (Chiapas sage). Both are moderately sized growers with 'Wendy's Wish' growing 3 feet (90 cm) tall and wide, and *S. chiapensis* being somewhat smaller. They have in common brilliantly colored flowers in shades of fuchsia pink to red, and they bloom all summer into fall.

With its masses of intense scarlet flowers, the well-known *Salvia elegans* is frequently planted in climates outside of its comfort zone (Zone 9a), though it does not bloom until early autumn. Other salvias to try in the pink to red range are *S. curviflora*, selections of *S. involucrata*, and *S. puberula* 'El Butano'.

LUSH FOLIAGE

A lush tropical look in a cold-climate garden is possible by using some of the large-leaved salvias. The upright form of *Salvia macrophylla* with its large, pointed, triangular leaves is unique, and its purple-leaved form is particularly striking with the underside of the leaves strongly veined and brushed with bronzy purple. The large, rich blue flowers, while very impressive, take a back seat to the leaves.

Purple-stemmed *Salvia madrensis* 'Red Neck Girl' also adds boldness to a border. The strongly angular, square stems have prominent corners, like buttresses on old cathedrals, seemingly designed by an engineer for added strength.

Salvia confertiflora adds foliage interest to a border. It has a strong upright habit with richly textured leaves held by orange-red petioles that are complementary to the long, narrow spires of small, closely set orange flowers. If uninhibited by frost, the flowers are appropriately seasonal in mid to late autumn. The leaves of *S. caudata* 'El Cielo Blue', while neither big nor bold, are particularly deep green on a dense plant that brings a fresh lushness to any planting.

Bringing more salvias into the garden as annual plants opens a world of design options. The range of flower color is phenomenal giving the gardener a broad color palette from which to choose. In most climates, salvias will not be structural plants in the garden, but instead will be seasonal accents to bring brightness, texture, and life that enhance the garden in summer and fall.

Herb Gardens

Salvias are at home in any herb garden style. Dating back to ancient historic monastery and teaching gardens, the traditional herb garden was a formal, often contained, and well-organized garden space. Today, herb gardens come in all shapes, sizes, and styles. Casual, naturalistic herb gardens can be every bit as pleasing and functional as the more traditional formal parterre garden, depending on your taste.

The Mediterranean salvias, or sages as they are usually called in culinary and therapeutic contexts, are most frequently used in herb gardens, with *Salvia officinalis* and all its forms being perhaps the most commonly seen and the easiest to grow. The plants can be tall and generously spreading or, if pruned, can be used as controlled edging, in which role the cultivars sporting purple or variegated leaves make nice accents. Garden sages bring foliage and flowers into the garden, along with the leaves and essential oils used in cooking.

Other salvias used for culinary and medicinal purposes include *Salvia lavandulifolia* (Spanish sage) and *S. fruticosa* (Greek sage). Both of these species yield more essential oil than common culinary sage does, and the oils are particularly prized for scenting soaps and perfumes. Writing in their *Encyclopedia of Herbs*, Arthur O. Tucker and Thomas Debaggio noted that upwards of 95 percent of all the dried, imported cooking sage sold in the United Stares is *S. fruticosa*. Both sage species, like many others, offer nice aesthetic additions to the herb garden: Spanish sage provides a more casual but still tidy clumping form and cheerful lavender-blue flowers, while Greek sage offers a formal, rigid verticality in its stalks covered from top to bottom in furry little divided leaves.

Another salvia mainstay for the herb garden is *Salvia sclarea*, whose common name clary sage refers to the plant's traditional use in treating vision matters (from the word *clary* suggesting "clear"). According to the *Encyclopedia of Herbs*, clary sage is often used to flavor wines and other specialty alcohols, and its foliage, flowers, and persistent colorful bracts provide a striking visual addition to the herb garden as well.

Salvias That Attract Bees

GORDON FRANKIE IS a professor and research entomologist at the University of California, Berkeley, where he oversees the Urban Bee Project, a statewide project devoted to monitoring native bee populations in urban environments. Gordon's top five salvias for attracting native bees are as follows:
Salvia brandegeei
Salvia 'Indigo Spires'
Salvia leucophylla
Salvia mellifera
Salvia uliginosa

Other good salvias that attract bees include the following:
Salvia 'Anthony Parker'
Salvia 'Bee's Bliss'
Salvia lavandulifolia
Salvia melissodora
Salvia 'Mystic Spires Blue'
Salvia officinalis
Salvia ringens
Salvia ×*sylvestris* cultivars
Salvia transsylvanica

Salvia confertiflora is grown for its wonderful textured foliage and its striking late summer to fall flowers.

Two forms of *Salvia officinalis* lend foliage texture, color, and fragrance in an herb garden.

In the herb garden at Denver Botanic Gardens, *Salvia officinalis* blooms in late spring.

Large, red square stems are prominent in *Salvia madrensis* 'Red Neck Girl'.

048_Sclevelandii_EmilyGreen_JW_Caut.tif-
CMYK
300
100%

In Containers

Many salvias both hardy and tender are well suited to being planted in containers, which, when placed on decks or patios, allow the floral colors, foliage texture, and humming-birds they attract to be enjoyed more closely. The large pot of *Salvia* 'Wendy's Wish' growing on my deck, for example, is positioned so that I can enjoy its long season of rosy red flowers from inside the house, along with the Anna's hummingbird who frequents the flowers and the buzzing carpenter bees who accompany my summertime early morning cup of coffee.

Any number of small salvias can be incorporated into mixed plantings in large containers. Plants with textured foliage, such as *Salvia nana*, or *S. sinaloensis*, can provide textural interest along with cheerful flowers. The small forms of the always-in-bloom hybrids of *S. greggii* and *S. microphylla* can bring a whole range of colors from which to choose.

When pots of annual color are desired, gardeners can choose from many selections of *Salvia coccinea*, *S. farinacea* (mealy cup sage), or *S. splendens* (scarlet sage). If a large, bold plant is needed to anchor a group of pots, try *S. guaranitica*, or *S. involucrata*. The choices are many when considering planting salvias in containers.

When she established young fruit trees in her Altadena (California) garden, Emily Green also planted *Salvia clevelandii* to encourage pollinators to visit the trees in bloom.

A well-grown *Salvia invo-lucrata* at the Los Angeles County Arboretum in a large formal container should flower through summer and fall.

Hummingbirds are not just attracted to red; they are frequent visitors to the blue flowers of *Salvia guaranitica*.

In a Wildlife Garden

Salvias are important plants to include in any garden where wildlife, in its infinite variety, is encouraged. Sitting by a bank of blooming *Salvia* 'Bee's Bliss' one spring I was immersed in the diversity of life that was drawn into its midst. Multitudes of pipevine swallowtails—perhaps a hundred—flitted, floated, and drifted among the vertical stems of lavender-blue flowers with the noticeable sound—the low sonorous harmonics—of hundreds of bumblebees enriching the experience. Besides the plentiful swallowtails and bumblebees, monarchs, honeybees, and a number of solitary native bees were part of this lively scene. While it is not a common experience to have such an abundance of wildlife attending one planting, it is rare to walk past any salvia without disturbing at least one creature—a syrphid fly, honeybee, native bee, butterfly, or hummingbird.

Many first-time growers of salvias do so after researching the best plants for attracting hummingbirds. Salvias have a dependable reputation for bringing and keeping hummingbirds around the garden. Visitors to a garden planted with salvias can be amazed and overwhelmed by the high energy of hummingbirds defending their favorite plant.

This added life attracted into the garden not only generates energy and beauty for human enjoyment but also makes for healthier gardens. Many benefits result from bringing more insect life into a garden. Yields in vegetable and fruit production increase because there are more pollinators to do the pollinating. Studies show that the greater the diversity of flowering plants, the greater the diversity of insect populations which help maintain a healthy balance in a garden. Beneficial insects assist in keeping not-so-welcome insects in check. For instance, the larvae of syrphid flies feed voraciously on aphids. The more syrphid flies, the fewer aphids. Insects attracted into the garden are also a source of food for predators—large and small.

A syrphid fly visiting a salvia.

A honeybee gathers nectar from *Salvia leucophylla*.

A carpenter bee drinks nectar from *Salvia* 'Wendy's Wish'.

UNDERSTANDING SALVIAS

S*alvia* is the largest genus in the Lamiaceae, or mint family, comprising roughly 900 species and many hundreds of horticultural selections and hybrids. The range of plant size, flower size, flower color, foliage form, and hardiness within the genus is tremendous. It includes annuals, biennials, perennials, and both evergreen and deciduous woody species. In the 1917 edition of *Standard Cyclopedia of Horticulture*, the editors acknowledged the size of this genus: "Within the generic limits of salvia, the variation is astonishing." At the time this was written, the genus was thought to comprise about 500 species.

The common denominator that connects all salvias and brings them into a single genus is the flower structure. Like all plants in the mint family, salvias share three basic visual traits: opposite leaves, square stems, and bilaterally symmetrical flowers (having two sides that are mirror images of each other). They also share one not-so-visible trait: bisexual flowers (having both male and female parts). What makes salvias unique from other mint family members is that the corolla tube (the petals) is two lipped, the upper and lower lip being significantly different from each other. The arrangement of the two stamens (the male pollen-producing organs) is also a key identifier.

The tiny clump form of *Salvia muirii*, a South Africa native, is haloed by its succulent dryland garden companions in Corralitos, California, in the garden of salvia enthusiast Sandi Martin.

Distribution

The great diversity of salvias is due to their adaptations through time to varied geographical origins and habitats. Salvias are found on almost every continent: in North America (20 species), Central (300 species) and South America (220 species), throughout Europe, especially around the Mediterranean (250 species), into Asia (90 species), and a few in South Africa (30 species). This is a genus well travelled.

A sizeable portion of salvias are native to the New World, a handful of these being from California through the Southwest across to Texas. An increasing number are found as you head south throughout Mexico, Central and South America. Some of the showiest salvias, those with intense brilliant colors, originate from this region. While many of these are tender, tropical species, others come from the mountainous regions of Mexico and include relatively hardy species such as *Salvia darcyi*, *S. greggii*, *S. microphylla*, and *S. regla*.

Eurasia is home to some of the most cold-tolerant salvias for gardens, including the parent species of the popular *Salvia* ×*sylvestris* cultivars, as well as *S. verticillata* 'Purple Rain'. Coarse, often hairy, green leaves and short spikes of open-mouthed flowers are typical of this group of salvias. They are found growing in meadows, on steep mountain slopes, and in open woodlands.

Included in the Eurasian group are the often slightly less winter hardy Mediterranean salvias. Turkey boasts nearly 50 endemic species of salvias. Drought tolerance and fragrant silver or gray foliage are frequent traits of many of the Mediterranean salvias, including the iconic cooking sage, *Salvia officinalis*. The foliage of these species has evolved to survive hot, dry, cold conditions and the intense grazing of animals where forage is limited. Often there are hairs on the leaves to reflect the heat of the sun and reduce

Cold-tolerant *Salvia ×sylvestris* 'Caradonna' is derived from a European species and is grown for its pleasing vertical flower spikes.

transpiration. Most salvias contain a blend of volatile fragrant oils along with having sticky inflorescences to discourage grazing—all adaptations for survival.

Another handful of salvias call South Africa home. Like the tropical species, they generally have little tolerance for cold temperatures. This group includes some striking and variable salvias. For example, *Salvia lanceolata* has stiff silver foliage and unusual, large rusty orange-brown flowers, while fine-textured *S. muirii* displays tiny green leaves and very pretty, comparatively large light blue flowers. Many of the South African salvias, like plants of the California chaparral, are adapted to periodic wildfires and will grow from the base of the plant after a fire moves through.

A voracious Anna's hummingbird plunges its beak deep into the corolla tube of a *Salvia mexicana*. You can see the pollen-laden stamen brushing the visiting pollinator's head.

Pollination Partners

Most salvias have a unique means of pollination—quite incredible in fact. It involves the teeter-totter action of the stamen filaments in what is described as the *staminal lever mechanism*. This clever adaptation ensures ripe pollen is placed on the appropriate pollinator, be it a bee, sunbird, moth, or hummingbird.

The staminal lever mechanism provides a mechanical way for the flower to deposit a bit of pollen on the visiting pollinator. This action is particularly noticeable when a hummingbird visits one of the salvias with a tubular flower. The hummingbird inserts its beak into the flower to sip the nectar at the flower's base. The beak pushes against a hinged filament, which acts like a teeter-totter and forces the stamens down onto the head of the hummingbird. In the process, the stamens deposit a dab of pollen on the hummingbird. The pollen is carried by the hummingbird to the next flower and, if the flower's stigma hangs down conveniently at the right level for the hummingbird's head to brush against it, the pollen is transferred.

Salvias have evolved this intriguing method of pollination to match the region of the world where they are found. In the Old World (Eurasia), salvia flowers are shaped for bee pollination. These flowers usually have an extended lower lip for the bee to land on, often marked with a "bee guide" (see photo of *Salvia sinaloensis* on page 166), and a relatively shorter corolla tube. Entering the flower for nectar, the bee pushes against the stamen filaments and, like the action of a teeter-totter, the stamens with ripe pollen are lowered against the back or side of the bee.

New World salvias, particularly those in Central and South America where hummingbirds live, have developed a rewarding symbiotic relationship between flower and pollinator. To match the hummingbird's long slender bill, salvia flowers have evolved a long corolla tube, a sugar-rich nectar for enticement, and a longer stamen filament. When I have dissected flowers to view more closely the staminal lever mechanism, I have been awed by the diversity of adaptations that plants in general, and salvias in particular, have made. Plants and pollinators have worked out a mutually beneficial system.

150 SALVIAS FOR THE GARDEN

Salvia africana-caerulea

This densely branched shrub has semideciduous leaves that are small, thick, and covered with fine hairs. The flowers are large compared to the leaf size, a lovely lavender-blue with the broad lower lip slightly lighter in color. The calyces are purplish.

TYPE, HABIT, AND SIZE A tender shrub to 4 feet (1.2 m) tall and nearly as wide.
HARDINESS Zone 9b
ORIGIN South Africa
CULTIVATION Treat like other South African or Mediterranean sages by ensuring good drainage and not overwatering in the growing season. Grow it in full sun.
LANDSCAPE USE With its naturally dense nature, this salvia makes a fine informal hedge or screen in mild climates. A lone plant blends easily into a Mediterranean- or Southwest-style garden.

Salvia amarissima

A gentle, easy-to-grow shrub that produces long spikes of flowers from late spring into fall. The flowers are sky blue with a large lip that seemingly cascades down the flowering stem.

TYPE, HABIT, AND SIZE A tender shrub 4–5 feet (1.2–1.5 m) tall and 4 feet (1.2 m) wide.
HARDINESS Zone 9b
ORIGIN Central America
CULTIVATION Grows best in moisture-retentive soils with afternoon shade.
LANDSCAPE USE In a woodland or shady mixed border.

Salvia 'Amistad'▸

Introduced in 2012 as part of *Sunset Magazine*'s Western Garden Collection. First-year experiences have been very positive, making 'Amistad' a wonderful new addition to the salvia world. Compact light green leaf growth with full spikes of deep purple flowers emerging from the glossy purple-black calyces that open over a long season.

TYPE, HABIT, AND SIZE A half-hardy perennial 3–5 feet (0.9–1.5 m) tall and 3 feet (0.9 m) wide.
HARDINESS Zone 9a. The cultivar has not been in cultivation long enough to get a true sense of its hardiness.
ORIGIN A selection from Argentina
CULTIVATION Same culture as *S. guaranitica* hybrids. These leafy plants appreciate a bit of shade in hot climates, regular water, and compost-enriched soil. Removing spent flowers and trimming the plant lightly during the growing season encourages flowering.
LANDSCAPE USE An easy salvia to tuck in a perennial or shrub border wherever lush purple flowers are desired. It is an excellent choice for a container.

Salvia 'Anthony Parker'▸

Extremely floriferous beginning in early fall, 'Anthony Parker' bears long, narrow spikes of deep indigo blue flowers. The narrow leaves have a slight silver-gray cast, though in general resemble the venation of *S. elegans* leaves—without the scent. A good bee and butterfly plant.

TYPE, HABIT, AND SIZE A tender perennial 4–5 feet (1.2–1.5 m) tall and 4–6 feet (1.2–1.8 m) wide.
HARDINESS Zone 9b
ORIGIN A chance hybrid, perhaps between *S. leucantha* 'Midnight' and *S. elegans*.
CULTIVATION Easy to grow in full sun with regular water.
LANDSCAPE USE Plant with other late-season perennials, such as asters, helianthus, rudbeckias, and large grasses for a lively, colorful end to the season.

Salvia apiana ◂
White sage

White sage is appropriately named for its prominent silvery white leaves and wands of white flowers. The Latin name *apiana* indicates the plant's attractiveness to bees. The flower is seemingly designed for a larger pollinator than the European honeybee, which works hard getting into the constricted opening to reach the nectar. Bumblebees or the large carpenter bees are a better match for this California native. White sage can be a compact shrub; however, this compactness is deceiving as the flower stems can rise 4 feet (1.2 m) above the plant, exploding in all directions. The leaves are powerfully fragrant.

TYPE, HABIT, AND SIZE An evergreen, rounded shrub 3–4 feet (90–120 cm) tall before flowering, with flowering stems 6–8 feet (1.8–2.4 m) tall.
HARDINESS Zone 8b
ORIGIN California
CULTIVATION A candidate for the dry garden where it thrives in poor, well-drained soils. It seems particularly sensitive to wet winter conditions or excessive water in the summer. Cut back the long flower stems for a more compact, tidier plant. Grow it in full sun.
LANDSCAPE USE The silvery whiteness of foliage and flowers makes this salvia a strong focal point when set against the green of xeric shrubs such as ceanothus, coffeeberry, and arctostaphylos. White sage is also very reflective with night lighting.

Salvia argentea

Silver sage

Silver sage produces a wide and low rosette of appealingly ruffled and woolly basal foliage the first year. This intricate web of soft, silvery white hairs makes it a frequently photographed sage and a lovely textural accent in the garden. In its second year of growth, it sends up tall, branched flower stems. It has a propensity to seed about.

TYPE, HABIT, AND SIZE A hardy perennial with a clump of basal leaves to 24 inches (60 cm) across and flowering stems to 30 inches (75 cm) tall.

HARDINESS Zone 6a

ORIGIN Southern Europe, North Africa.

CULTIVATION As suggested by its hairy foliage, silver sage is used to growing in full sun. It needs well-drained soil and limited amounts of water. Some gardeners recommend removing the flowers soon after they open to prevent seed production and thus extend the life of the plant. Others enjoy the airy panicles of hooded white flowers until they fade.

LANDSCAPE USE This salvia is attractive toward the front of the border where its felted leaves can be viewed up close. It provides a stunning contrast of color and texture in the garden.

Salvia aurea

Beach sage

SYNONYM *Salvia africana-lutea*

Similar to *S. africana-caerulea* with its wiry dense growth and small thick fragrant leaves. The flowers, however, are different, those of this species large and yellow, arranged in terminal whorled clusters that quickly fade to a rich burnt sienna. It is the intense aging color of the flower that one associates with the plant, along with the long-lasting calyces, which in some selections can also be quite colorful.

TYPE, HABIT, AND SIZE A tender shrub 4–5 feet (1.2–1.5 m) tall and 4–6 feet (1.2–1.8 m) wide.

HARDINESS Zone 9b

ORIGIN South Africa.

CULTIVATION Plenty of sun, good drainage, occasional water.

LANDSCAPE USE Place along a path, though not necessarily front and forward, where the subtle colors of its ever-changing flowers and bracts can be appreciated.

RELATED PLANTS

'Kirstenbosch' A more floriferous selection of *S. aurea*.

Salvia azurea var. *grandiflora*

Pitcher sage

Beautiful sky blue flowers and an ungainly habit come to mind when thinking of the pitcher sage. The plant grows upright until midsummer when the stems become more lax, wanting to rest on nearby companions. The flowers are a lovely shade of powdery blue. The long, narrow leaves are a grayish green.

TYPE, HABIT, AND SIZE A hardy perennial 3–5 feet (0.9–1.5 m) tall and 3 feet (0.9 m) wide.

HARDINESS Zone 4

ORIGIN South-central United States.

CULTIVATION Adaptable to varying water regimes and soils, it is not a fussy plant. Grow in partial to full sun. Cut it back in late spring or early summer for a fuller plant.

LANDSCAPE USE As with people, it is usually best not to try to modify a plant's inherent nature; accepting and working with the strengths of a person or a plant is often a wiser path. With this in mind, situate the pitcher sage knowing that it will sprawl over nearby plants when it begins to bloom. Choose companion plants that will mingle happily and will not mind becoming entwined by late summer. Several grasses work well along with the taller rudbeckias, solidago, and helianthus.

RELATED PLANTS

'Nekan' A seed strain from a population in Nebraska-Kansas (hence the name) reputed to have a more robust nature and slightly larger flowers.

Salvia 'Bee's Bliss'

This evergreen shrub sends out sweeping branches that make a lush carpet of narrow gray-green leaves. The stems take root along the ground. Planted in the spring, 'Bee's Bliss' can easily spread 4 feet (1.2 m) the first season with little water. Blooming in late spring and early summer, it produces whorls of light lavender-blue flowers. And of course, as the name suggests, it is highly attractive to bees.

TYPE, HABIT, AND SIZE An evergreen groundcover 18 inches (45 cm) tall and spreading 6–8 feet (1.8–2.4 m) across.

HARDINESS Zone 8b

ORIGIN A supposed hybrid of California native sages *S. leucophylla* and *S. sonomensis*, originating from the University of California Botanical Garden at Berkeley.

CULTIVATION Thrives in full sun with very little irrigation. In the fall or late winter, cut back to remove old flowers and any excessively lanky growth.

LANDSCAPE USE For covering the ground quickly on poor soils in full sun and with little irrigation, 'Bee's Bliss' is an excellent choice. It excels at covering exposed banks. In the dry garden, it combines readily with other large drought-tolerant plants. It can provide an attractive contrast to baccharis, cistus, ceanothus, other substantial salvias, or weaving in and out of large grasses such as deer grass (*Muhlenbergia rigens*; see photo on page 24), or between large rocks.

Salvia 'Big Swing'

An excellent hybrid with lush, large green leaves composing a low-growing clump. Arising from the foliage are numerous branched stalks of flowers carrying some of the most cobalt, electric blue flowers imaginable.

TYPE, HABIT, AND SIZE A tender perennial with the foliage growing 18 inches (45 cm) tall and the flowers 18–24 inches (45–60 cm) above that. The plant grows several feet across.

HARDINESS Zone 10a

ORIGIN A chance seedling between *S. macrophylla* and *S. sagittata*.

CULTIVATION With its luxuriant growth, this plant needs adequate water and fertilizer. Too much nitrogen, however, will result in fewer flowers. The plant also requires some shade in hot, sunny climates.

LANDSCAPE USE Fast growth makes this salvia a good choice for a container plant or even a filler in a perennial border in all climates, where a long season of clear blue flowers is desired.

Salvia blepharophylla

Eyelash leaf sage

Glossy, bright green leaves, intense scarlet flowers, and a manageable habit make *S. blepharophylla* highly desirable. The flowers are saturated with brilliant color as if they were dipped in a pot of paint. While never making an all-out burst of color, this sage always displays a smattering of flowers to bring some cheerful color to a shady part of the garden. The plant spreads slowly by rhizomatous roots. The common name reflects the fine hairs that edge the leaf.

TYPE, HABIT, AND SIZE A half-hardy perennial 18–24 inches (45–60 cm) tall and 4 feet (1.2 m) wide.

HARDINESS Zone 9a

ORIGIN Northeastern Mexico

CULTIVATION Prefers a shady situation, especially in hot summer climates, and a well-drained, yet moisture-retentive soil. Thin stems and remove old flowers as needed during the growing season. Remove any winter dieback in early spring.

LANDSCAPE USE Easily used along a path as an underplanting to larger shrubs or small trees.

RELATED PLANTS

'Diablo' A selection with yellow stamens prominent against the scarlet petals.

'Painted Lady' ▶ The leaves have a purple cast, making the eyelash hairs more evident on this selection.

Salvia brandegeei 'Pacific Blue'◂

A fine selection of one of California's native sages having narrow, pebbled deep green leaves and deeply colored lavender-blue flowers in small whorls set along the 2-foot (60-cm) tall flowering stems. A good landscape plant with its dark green foliage and richly colored flowers.

TYPE, HABIT, AND SIZE An evergreen shrub 3–4 feet (0.9–1.2 m) tall and 5–6 feet (1.5–1.8 m) across.

HARDINESS Zone 8b

ORIGIN A seedling found and introduced by the Santa Barbara Botanic Garden.

CULTIVATION Extremely drought tolerant, so be careful not to overwater in summer or winter. It is suggested that this cultivar is tolerant of heavier soils. In early fall, cut back the old flower stalks and maybe a fourth of the foliage if a more compact plant is desired.

LANDSCAPE USE Effective for planting on banks and hillsides with other California natives, such as coffeeberry, white sage, and baccharis.

Salvia buchananii▾

Buchanan's sage

Buchanan's sage is a small plant with glossy, leathery, deep green leaves on slender, often lax stems. While never produced in mass, the large, glowing magenta flowers stand out against the rich green background of the foliage.

TYPE, HABIT, AND SIZE A half-hardy perennial 18 inches (45 cm) tall and 12–18 inches (30–45 cm) wide.

HARDINESS Zone 9b

ORIGIN Mexico

CULTIVATION Prefers a soil amended with compost. Needs regular irrigation during the growing season. A sheltered position with relief from the hot afternoon sun is best.

LANDSCAPE USE A perfect candidate for container culture.

Salvia cacaliifolia ▸

Guatemalan leaf sage

Leafy, spreading, and mixing it up with its neighbors, Guatemalan leaf sage is usually not seen alone, but in the context of other plants. New growth is often erect, but soon takes a turn to the horizontal. The leaves are slightly hairy, with a strongly defined deltoid, or arrow shape. The clear, gentian-blue flowers open on the branched inflorescence in summer and fall.

TYPE, HABIT, AND SIZE A tender perennial 2–4 feet (0.6–1.2 m) tall and 4–6 feet (1.2–1.8 m) wide.
HARDINESS Zone 10a
ORIGIN Central America
CULTIVATION Easily grown in good friable soil with regular watering in summer. Afternoon shade is necessary in hot summer climates. Cut back in the growing season as needed.
LANDSCAPE USE In milder climates where *S. cacaliifolia* is perennial, plant among shrubs or sturdy perennials that support its scandent habit. In colder climates use as a container plant where the trailing leafy growth and bright blue flowers will enhance a mixed container grouping.

Salvia caespitosa ▸

One of a handful of salvias considered appropriate for a true rock garden setting, *S. caespitosa* makes a tight cushion of grayish green ferny foliage. Nestled against the fine foliage, the white to pale pink flowers seem large relative to the diminutive scale of the plant.

TYPE, HABIT, AND SIZE A hardy perennial 6 inches (15 cm) tall and 18 inches (45 cm) wide.
HARDINESS Zone 5
ORIGIN Turkey
CULTIVATION A sunny position and very well drained soils are the keys to success with this salvia. Be careful not to overwater in summer; plant with a top layer of gravel, which allows for good aeration.
LANDSCAPE USE Besides use in the rock garden, this salvia is well suited for container culture.

Salvia canariensis▲

Canary Island sage

A vigorous, robust shrub, Canary Island sage is quite dramatic. Its woolly silvery white foliage and big stems carry showy clusters of lilac-pink flowers set in deeper colored calyces and leaf bracts. Even after the flowers drop, the bracts and calyces extend the colorful display for months.

TYPE, HABIT, AND SIZE A half-hardy shrub 6–7 feet (1.8–2.1 m) tall and 5–7 feet (1.5–2.1 m) wide.
HARDINESS Zone 8b
ORIGIN Canary Islands
CULTIVATION Easily cultivated, this sage is adaptable, only requiring a place in the sun. It can tolerate being grown on the dry side, but additional water will result in a larger plant. Cut back hard in early spring to encourage new growth.
LANDSCAPE USE Best used as a background accent plant where it can attain full size. In mild climates, it makes a colorful hedge. Place where morning or evening light will ignite the brilliantly colored bracts.

Salvia candelabrum

In late spring or early summer, long, branched flowering stems emerge from a low, shrubby mound of gray-green foliage carrying quantities of large violet-blue flowers veined with white. The combination makes for an impressive, long-lasting, airy display.

TYPE, HABIT, AND SIZE A woody-based evergreen perennial, forming a mound of foliage 30 inches (75 cm) tall and wide, with flowering stems to 5 feet (1.5 m) tall.
HARDINESS Zone 7b
ORIGIN Spain
CULTIVATION Reasonably adaptable. Should grow wherever *S. officinalis* grows. Prefers good drainage and not being overwatered. Remove old flower stalks if desired.
LANDSCAPE USE At home in a mixed border of perennials and roses.
SIMILAR PLANTS
Salvia interrupta Similar to *S. candelabrum* but smaller growing.

Salvia 'Carl Nielson'

While not commonly seen in the nursery trade and with a reputation for being temperamental, this hybrid is still a stunning plant when well grown. Its leaves are similar to those of *S. clevelandii*, a possible parent, but greener. The flowers are a rich violet-blue enhanced by darker bracts. The whorled inflorescence dries to a deep tan and is prominent long after the flowers fade.

TYPE, HABIT, AND SIZE A semihardy evergreen shrub 3 feet (0.9 m) tall and wide.
HARDINESS Zone 8a
ORIGIN Thought to be a hybrid between California sages *S. clevelandii* and *S. mohavensis*.
CULTIVATION In one garden where I planted several plants of 'Carl Nielsen', surprisingly the one nearest the lawn sprinklers did significantly better. The parentage would suggest this hybrid needs lean and dry growing conditions, but it seems some extra watering might be appreciated.
LANDSCAPE USE With its compact size, this salvia is easy to use with xeric perennials such as eriogonum, nepeta, penstemon, or zauschneria.

Salvia caudata
'El Cielo Blue'

Blue sky Mexican sage

Clean, heart-shaped leaves with attractive veining give this salvia a fresh, lush look during the growing season. The flowers are quite beautiful—a dark lavender-blue with two brushstrokes of white on the lower lip. Blue sky Mexican sage may not be a showstopping salvia, but it is a very attractive addition.

TYPE, HABIT, AND SIZE A tender perennial 3-5 feet (0.9–1.5 m) tall and wide.
HARDINESS Zone 10a
ORIGIN Mexico
CULTIVATION Grows readily in a moisture-retentive soil with regular water and some relief from the hot sun in warmer climates.
LANDSCAPE USE A good container plant where it can be a counterpoint for bolder foliage or variegated plants. The flowers are lovely when seen up close.

Salvia chamaedryoides ▲
Germander sage

Germander sage forms a small shrublet with thin woody stems clothed in diminutive silvery gray leaves. The pretty, deep blue flowers are carried on slender scapes from late spring into fall. With a slowly spreading rootstock, the plant continues to broaden its presence but is easily managed.

TYPE, HABIT, AND SIZE A semihardy evergreen shrub 18 inches (45 cm) tall and 36 inches (90 cm) wide.
HARDINESS Zone 7
ORIGIN Texas, Mexico
CULTIVATION Prefers full sun and well-drained soil, though it is not too fussy about the latter. Is reasonably drought tolerant.
LANDSCAPE USE Germander sage finds many homes in a garden. Because it is not showy from a distance, plant it in close, along a path or among a group of rocks, creating a niche where the fine silver foliage and blue flowers can be featured. Surround it with zauschneria, penstemon, lavender, and erigeron to make a colorful dry-cottage garden planting (see photo). Makes an excellent container plant. When planted on 30-inch (75-cm) centers and cut back hard in late winter, it makes a solid groundcover.

Salvia chamelaeagnea ▶
African blue sage

Congested, tightly packed, and dense are a few words to describe how the leaves and flowers are arranged on this shrubby salvia. The small leaves are substantive, slightly sticky, and tightly arranged on the square stems. The light lavender-blue flowers are set in whorls on a densely branched inflorescence with contrasting reddish purple calyces.

TYPE, HABIT, AND SIZE A tender evergreen shrub 4 feet (1.2 m) tall and 3–6 feet (0.9–1.8 m) wide.
HARDINESS Zone 9b
ORIGIN South Africa
CULTIVATION Needs sun and good drainage.
LANDSCAPE USE Because it is very much a textural plant, situate this sage with contrast in mind. Selected larger leaved plants make particularly good companions.

Salvia chiapensis
Chiapas sage

While I have never had success with Chiapas sage in my own hot interior California garden, I have seen it looking carefree and floriferous in many other gardens. The small, bright fuchsia-pink flowers are cheerful and long blooming, produced generously on the 12- to 18-inch (30- to 45-cm) stems that rise and lean outward above the bright green glossy foliage.

TYPE, HABIT, AND SIZE A tender perennial 2–3 feet (0.6–0.9 m) tall and 3–4 feet (0.9–1.2 m) wide.
HARDINESS Zone 10a
ORIGIN Chiapas (state) in Mexico.
CULTIVATION Plant in well-drained, compost-enhanced soil and provide regular water during the growing season.
LANDSCAPE USE Use above low walls and along pathways where its leaning nature will soften edges. Grows well in containers.

Salvia chionophylla
Snowflake sage

A unique little salvia with thin trailing stems that lay on the ground. The new growth is a soft downy gray, and the small oval leaves are pistachio green with a hint of powdery gray. The small lavender-blue flowers are held on short stems just above the foliage.

TYPE, HABIT, AND SIZE An evergreen perennial 6 inches (15 cm) tall and 30 inches (75 cm) wide.
HARDINESS Zone 9b
ORIGIN Mexico
CULTIVATION Needs good drainage with occasional summer water. Grow it in full sun to light shade.
LANDSCAPE USE Clearly a small-scale groundcover, suited for mixed container plantings or trailing over low retaining walls.

Salvia 'Christine Yeo'

'Christine Yeo' is a dependable, floriferous salvia. The flowers, a blend of lavender, violet, and pink with a touch of white in the throat, are changeable with the light. This long-blooming, compact grower spreads slowly over time.

TYPE, HABIT, AND SIZE A woody perennial 18 inches (45 cm) tall and 3 feet (90 cm) wide.

HARDINESS Zone 8

ORIGIN A garden hybrid between *S. chamaedryoides* and *S. microphylla*.

CULTIVATION Grow it in full to partial sun in well-drained soil.

LANDSCAPE USE Useful for the front of a perennial border, alongside pathways, or planted in groups of 3 and repeated throughout the landscape for a rhythm of color.

Salvia clevelandii
Cleveland sage

In California, particularly the southern part of the state, Cleveland sage is almost ubiquitous. It can be found growing in home gardens as well as in many commercial and public plantings. The reason for its popularity is clear: it has a tidy year-round presence, attractive flowers, low water requirements, and attracts bees, butterflies, and hummingbirds. This rounded, woody shrub is clothed in narrow gray-green leaves, whose fragrance is so eloquently described by Joan Walters as a waterfall of pungent aromas. The plant blooms profusely from late spring through midsummer with whorls of pretty blue-violet flowers.

TYPE, HABIT, AND SIZE An evergreen shrub 4–6 feet (1.2–1.8 m) tall and 4–7 feet (1.2–2.1 m) wide.

HARDINESS Zone 8

ORIGIN Southern California

CULTIVATION Good drainage, particularly in the winter, lean soil, and limited irrigation in the growing season.

LANDSCAPE USE Provides strong year-round form in any xeric garden.

RELATED PLANTS

'Aromas' A durable selection or hybrid of *S. clevelandii* growing 5 feet (1.5 m) tall and wide.

'Pozo Blue' An excellent selection or hybrid of *S. clevelandii*, tolerant of many growing conditions. Grows 3 feet (0.9 m) tall and wide.

'Vicki Romo' A lavender-flowered hybrid of *S. apiana* and *S. clevelandii* (see photo on page 30). The silver foliage resembles that of *S. apiana*.

'Whirley Blue' A strong-growing selection or hybrid of *S. clevelandii* with midblue flowers. Grows 5 feet (1.5 m) tall and wide. Perhaps the largest flowers of the cultivars.

Salvia clevelandii 'Winifred Gilman'

A very showy selection. The flowers, in well-spaced whorls, are a brilliant purplish blue held just above the dark green foliage. Distinctive and smaller than the other Cleveland sage cultivars.

TYPE, HABIT, AND SIZE A rounded evergreen shrub 3–5 feet (0.9–1.5 m) tall and wide, in time.
HARDINESS Zone 8b
ORIGIN California
CULTIVATION As with all the California native sages, 'Winifred Gilman' requires minimum irrigation during the growing season. Grow it in full sun in well-drained soil. Cut back the old flowering stems in fall and prune the woody stems lightly. The plant does not respond well to hard pruning.
LANDSCAPE USE 'Winifred Gilman' is a beautiful, showy plant to use in a large or small xeric landscape. It is very effective when surrounded by silver-leaved plants such as *Santolina chamaecyparissus* or *Artemisia canescens*.

Salvia coccinea

Scarlet sage

The scarlet sage has long been popular grown as an annual. It grows quickly from seed and flowers from early summer well into fall. The flowers, typically a bright scarlet red, are carried in a terminal raceme, and are a favorite of hummingbirds. Will frequently self-sow in the garden.

TYPE, HABIT, AND SIZE A tender perennial 2–3 feet (60–90 cm) tall and 18 inches (45 cm) wide.

HARDINESS Zone 9b

ORIGIN South America

CULTIVATION Prefers a friable soil in full sun, or in partial shade in hotter climates. Reasonably drought tolerant or can tolerate moderate watering. Deadhead (remove old flowers) to encourage blooming, or cut back by half in midsummer to bring on a second flush of flowers.

LANDSCAPE USE Frequently planted to attract hummingbirds, scarlet sage is excellent in containers or mixed borders.

RELATED PLANTS

'Coral Nymph' Soft salmon-pink with white flowers on compact plants 18 inches (45 cm) tall.

'Lady in Red' ◀ Bright red flowers on plants 24–30 inches (60–75 cm) tall.

'Snow Nymph' White flowers.

Salvia coccinea 'Brenthurst'

This has always been my favorite of the *S. coccinea* cultivars. The peachy pink flowers produced late spring through fall are subtle, yet cheerful.

TYPE, HABIT, AND SIZE A tender perennial with an upright habit 2–3 feet (60–90 cm) tall and 18 inches (45 cm) wide.

HARDINESS Zone 9b

ORIGIN Mexico

CULTIVATION Prefers a friable soil in full sun; partial shade is ok in hotter climates. Reasonably drought tolerant but can also tolerate moderate watering. Deadhead (remove old flowers) to encourage blooming, or cut back by half in midsummer to bring on a second flush of flowers. Fast and easy to grow from seed.

LANDSCAPE USE Easily placed in a mixed border with annuals and perennials where soft color is desired. Long blooming, it is ideally suited for mixed container plantings as it does not take much room and can grow above or through companion plants.

Salvia columbariae
Chia

Chia is one of a few definitive annual salvias. This remarkable little plant is often found growing on steep gravel slopes where competition for water and nutrients is tough. The flowers are an intense indigo blue nestled in evenly spaced whorls of burgundy calyces that bristle with iridescent luster. Strongly vertical stems rise up from a low mat of deeply lobed, soft green foliage. Historically, chia was a food source for a number of Native American tribes. Currently the seeds of this sage and *Salvia hispanica* are popular as an extremely high source of omega-3 fatty acids.

TYPE, HABIT, AND SIZE An annual 12–24 inches (30–60 cm) tall and 8 inches (20 cm) wide.
HARDINESS Zone 7
ORIGIN California, Arizona, Utah, Mexico.
CULTIVATION Select a sunny position in soil that drains well. Sow seed directly in the garden in the fall.
LANDSCAPE USE Effectively planted among rocks where the small stature and strong form can be appreciated.

Salvia confertiflora

A stately and distinctively tropical-looking salvia with quilted leaves and lush, velvety flowers. The woody, upright stems are clothed with large textured leaves, with rusty colored undersides. In late summer through fall, the long terminal spikes are densely set with small, fuzzy, burnt orange flowers set in deep rusty-red calyces.

TYPE, HABIT, AND SIZE A tender shrub 6–10 feet (1.8–3.0 m) tall and 4–8 feet (1.2–2.4 m) wide.
HARDINESS Zone 10a
ORIGIN Brazil
CULTIVATION This fast-growing salvia appreciates humus-enriched soil and regular water, along with afternoon shade. The stems are brittle so plant it where support can be provided by other plants or use some judicious staking.
LANDSCAPE USE The combination of exotic textures and unusual flower color makes it a focal plant in a tropical setting or a large container. May need support/protection from winds.

Salvia corrugata

The glossy, pebbled-textured leaves are a feature of the appropriately named *S. corrugata*. The narrow 4-inch (10-cm) long leaves are deep green and densely clothe the shrub. The richly colored violet-blue flowers are held in tight clusters. This salvia has a distinctive appearance.

TYPE, HABIT, AND SIZE A tender shrub 4 feet (1.2 m) tall and 3–4 feet (0.9–1.2 m) wide.
HARDINESS Zone 9b
ORIGIN Colombia, Ecuador, Peru.
CULTIVATION Prefers a good soil, with regular irrigation and some shade in hotter climates.
LANDSCAPE USE Because of its compact nature and strong foliage, it is a good choice for containers or for providing textural contrast in mixed plantings. In mild climates, it even makes a tight hedge.

Salvia 'Costa Rican Blue'

A vigorous salvia, 'Costa Rican Blue' has strong woody stems and substantial, rich green leaves. The large, deep blue flowers open atop the tall stems beginning in early fall. I have always found the unfurling of the ample inflorescence to be dramatic.

TYPE, HABIT, AND SIZE A half-hardy perennial 8 feet (2.4 m) tall and 4–5 feet (1.2–1.5 m) wide.
HARDINESS Zone 9a
ORIGIN Costa Rica
CULTIVATION Grow in partial shade. Cutting back in midsummer will encourage branching and thus produce more flowers. It is a strong, upright grower.
LANDSCAPE USE Because it is tall and late blooming, place it in the back of a border with tall miscanthus, helianthus, solidago, and other late salvias.
RELATED PLANTS
'Omaha Gold' A sport of 'Costa Rican Blue' with the leaf margins generously suffused with creamy gold. By late summer, the variegation does fade.

Salvia curviflora

This is a floriferous, colorful salvia for summer and fall color. It makes quite a show with profuse quantities of tubular, bright—yet not florescent—fuchsia-pink flowers held on long graceful spikes. The lower lip of the flower curves under. Plants make a colony of vertical woody stems clothed densely with dark green substantive leaves.

TYPE, HABIT, AND SIZE A tender shrub 4–6 feet (1.2–1.8 m) tall and 3–4 feet (0.9–1.2 m) wide.
HARDINESS Zone 9b
ORIGIN Mexico
CULTIVATION Grow it in full sun with regular summer irrigation. Thin and prune during the growing season to keep it tidy, saving any major pruning for early spring when old stems may be removed or cut back to make a strong framework.
LANDSCAPE USE Because of its long season of showy flowers, this salvia is useful for seasonal color in colder climates. Plant it in a large container or in a mixed border. The clean, attractive foliage is an added bonus.

Salvia cyanescens ▲

A cloud of light lavender-blue describes the airy inflorescence when *S. cyanescens* is in full bloom. The large, open-mouthed flowers are set in rosy calyces and are evenly spaced on many-branched stems. The large basal leaves are a soft gray-green.

TYPE, HABIT, AND SIZE A hardy perennial with a basal leaf clump 10 inches (25 cm) tall and wide, flowering stems 1–2 feet (30–60 cm) tall and wide.
HARDINESS Zone 6
ORIGIN Iran, Turkey.
CULTIVATION A dryland species, *S. cyanescens* requires little irrigation and does best in lean, well-drained soil. It will seed if the flowering stems are not removed before seed is set.
LANDSCAPE USE Used to perfection in a nonirrigated parking strip in Denver (see photo on page 192), combining beautifully with yarrows, gaillardias, and iris.

Salvia daghestanica▾

Despite its small stature compared with most salvias, *S. daghestanica* has a strong presence. Against a flat mat of substantive silver leaves, the intense deep violet-blue flowers provide a strong complementary contrast. The flowers are held in few-flowered whorls set along the stem. This very rugged plant is worth growing for the foliage alone.

TYPE, HABIT, AND SIZE A hardy perennial 4 inches (10 cm) tall and 18 inches (45 cm) wide, with flowering stems 10 inches (25 cm) tall.
HARDINESS Zone 5
ORIGIN Caucasus
CULTIVATION A dryland species that grows best in lean, well-drained soils with occasional water. When growing in a container, top dress with gravel to improve drainage.
LANDSCAPE USE An accent plant for a rock garden, or as an edging plant along pathways in a dry garden. Does well in containers.

Salvia darcyi

Sizeable, clear orange-red flowers on erect stems borne proudly above light green foliage make this a very showy salvia that can hold its own in any planting. Because it is found growing at high elevations, *S. darcyi* is remarkably hardy for a species from Mexico. The light green, deltoid leaves are hairy, sticky to the touch, and bear an herbal-fruity fragrance when bruised. A colonizer, *S. darcyi* increases every year, though not enough to be a problem. The species and its hybrids are highly attractive to hummingbirds and bloom from summer well into fall.

TYPE, HABIT, AND SIZE A hardy perennial 4 feet (1.2 m) tall and 5 feet (1.5 m) wide.
HARDINESS Zone 6b
ORIGIN Mexico
CULTIVATION Grow it in full sun with good drainage. Cut back the species to the ground in early spring, but with the hybrids, leave 6 inches (15 cm) or so of the woody stems.
LANDSCAPE USE Whether used as an annual in cold climates or a perennial in warmer climates, this species and its hybrids do well in mixed borders, as long as the soil drains well.
RELATED PLANTS
'John Whittlesey' This very vigorous hybrid is a cross between *S. darcyi* and *S.* 'Hot Lips' (see photo on page 199). It is an extremely floriferous and flamboyant salvia with large scarlet flowers that bloom from early summer to late autumn. It grows 4 feet (1.2 m) tall and 4–5 feet (1.2–1.5 m) wide. I remember the day that nurseryman Mike Thiede brought me a 5-gallon (19-liter) pot of this seedling for my opinion. Before he even asked, I said, "That is a good salvia!"
'Scarlet Spires' A hybrid between *S.* 'Raspberry Delight' and *S. darcyi*. The stems are tall and erect, with coral-red flowers. This more compact version of *S. darcyi* grows 40 inches (100 cm) tall and 30 inches (75 cm) wide.
'Schoolhouse Red' A chance cross between *S. darcyi* and *S. microphylla* 'Wild Thing.' It has the reddest flowers of the group. Hardy in Zone 5.

Salvia desoleana

A casual-looking salvia that seems to belong in a courtyard under old olive trees. The large, rugose, fragrant leaves make strong handsome clumps that spread by rhizomatous roots. The tall stems have evenly spaced whorls of white flowers. It is the foliage that appeals to me.

TYPE, HABIT, AND SIZE A half-hardy perennial forming a leafy clump 3 feet (0.9 m) tall and 3–4 feet (0.9–1.2 m) wide.
HARDINESS Zone 8
ORIGIN Mediterranean
CULTIVATION Grow it in full sun in well-drained soil with some water in summer.
LANDSCAPE USE The large, bold foliage provides a strong contrast to many other plants and softens the edges of paving.

Salvia 'Desperado'

A large hybrid with a distinctive presence. The leaves are similar to those of *S. apiana*, only longer and a little narrower. The flowers are similar to those of *S. leucophylla*, but in much larger, denser whorls on longer flowering stems. When dried later in the season, the flowers bring to mind weapons used by knights in the middle ages. They are hefty.

TYPE, HABIT, AND SIZE A large, woody, evergreen shrub 6–10 feet (1.8–3.0 m) tall and wide.
HARDINESS Zone 8b
ORIGIN A hybrid of California natives *S. apiana* and *S. leucophylla*.
CULTIVATION Good drainage and little summer irrigation. Trim selectively in the fall or early spring.
LANDSCAPE USE A big, bold plant for big spaces.

Salvia discolor
Andean silver sage

This salvia appeals to many because of the dark purple, near black flowers. These seemingly shy flowers barely show themselves, exerted just beyond the flattened light green calyx that is dusted with silver. The lax stems are whitish on new growth, while the leaves are a shiny light green above with downy white hairs below. Flowering is sporadic in the summer and fall.

TYPE, HABIT, AND SIZE A tender evergreen perennial with loose growth 30 inches (75 cm) tall and wide.
HARDINESS Zone 9a
ORIGIN Peru
CULTIVATION Good soil amended with compost and regular irrigation. Prune as needed throughout the growing season, cutting back hard in early spring after frost.
LANDSCAPE USE Because of its loose habit, this sage is not easy to place in the garden. Growing it in a container might be most effective so that the surprisingly dark, subtle flowers can be enjoyed close at hand. A small trellis for holding up the branches is advantageous.

Salvia dolomitica

Salvia dolomitica is a handsome shrub to be grown in mild climates, where its dense habit of grayish green leaves can be a mainstay throughout the seasons. The flowers, though intricately marked and beautiful to view close-up, are not the reason for growing this salvia. It is for the plant's neat, rounded presence in the garden—to provide constancy through the seasons.

TYPE, HABIT, AND SIZE A tender shrubby plant 3–4 feet (0.9–1.2 m) tall and 3–5 feet (0.9–1.5 m) wide.
HARDINESS Zone 9a
ORIGIN South Africa
CULTIVATION A rugged plant requiring little but good drainage and occasional water during summer.
LANDSCAPE USE In mild climates, this salvia blends well with other drought-tolerant shrubs, such as ceanothus, baccharis, manzanita, and the California native sages.

Salvia dombeyi
Sacred Inca sage

This sage is one of those plants that some people make a mission of growing, and if successful, are proud of it. The scandent stems require support of other plants, a fence, or a trellis. The flowers are the longest in the genus *Salvia*, with the calyx and corolla measuring 4.5 inches (11 cm) long and dangling off the plant like chimes.

TYPE, HABIT, AND SIZE A tender vining shrub with climbing stems to 10 feet (3 m) long or longer.
HARDINESS Zone 10a
ORIGIN Peru, Bolivia.
CULTIVATION Not a plant for hot, dry climates. It likes cool, moist, frost-free conditions.
LANDSCAPE USE This is a specialty specimen plant and accordingly should be planted wherever its optimal growing conditions can be met.

Salvia dorisiana
Fruit-scented sage

Most salvias have fragrant oils in their leaves, stems, or inflorescences, and often the scents are pungent, herbal, or medicinal. *Salvia dorisiana*, however, has a sweet pineapple and peach scent, a blend of fruits, stronger than that of the frequently grown pineapple-scented *S. elegans*. The leaves are large and fuzzy, which encourages touching to release the scent. The large pink flowers open in winter and early spring.

TYPE, HABIT, AND SIZE A tender perennial with a leafy, upright habit to 3–5 feet (0.9–1.5 m) tall and wide.
HARDINESS Zone 10a
ORIGIN Honduras
CULTIVATION Grows best in compost-enriched soil with regular irrigation.
LANDSCAPE USE In milder climates, this salvia makes an attractive plant in a mixed border. It does well in a large container.

Salvia dorrii

Purple sage

I remember the first time I saw purple sage growing in its native habitat on a back road into Death Valley. I was ecstatic to smell the powerfully fragrant foliage and to see the tight clusters of intense rose-purple flowers. My kids were patient with me as I ooohed and aaahed and took many pictures. This woody plant is covered with small, intensely scented leaves and flowers that range from light blue to deep intense blue set against the burgundy whorls.

TYPE, HABIT, AND SIZE A hardy evergreen shrub 2–3 feet (0.6–0.9 m) tall and wide.

HARDINESS Zone 5

ORIGIN Great Basin Region of the western United States.

CULTIVATION Very well drained soil, full sun, and little water are the requirements. Cut back individual branches sparingly, only as needed to keep the plant tidy.

LANDSCAPE USE A superb plant for the xeric landscape, planted with buckwheat, penstemon, artemisia, and similar plants.

RELATED PLANTS

'Gayle Nielson' Synonym 'Trident'. An excellent hybrid similar to *S. dorrii* in foliage and habit but with deeply colored purple flowers. Parentage includes *S. clevelandii*, *S. dorrii*, and *S. mohavensis*.

Salvia 'Dyson's Joy'

A highly attractive bicolored salvia with the large lower petal very pale pink and the corolla tube and upper petal a bright rosy pink. Makes for a lovely combination.

TYPE, HABIT, AND SIZE A semievergreen woody subshrub to 2 feet (60 cm) tall and nearly as wide.
HARDINESS Zone 7b
ORIGIN A hybrid from the *Salvia greggii/microphylla* complex and an unnamed species.
CULTIVATION Grow it in full sun to light shade in well-drained soil. Trim lightly during the growing season, then prune hard (cut back halfway) in early spring.
LANDSCAPE USE Good in a container, a mixed border, or with roses.

Salvia elegans

Pineapple sage

Pineapple sage has been one of the most popular salvias through the years, whether grown as an annual in cold climates or a perennial in milder zones. The fragrance of the leaves—sweet and, yes, pineapple-like—is one reason to grow it, but most gardeners love it for its long display of scarlet flowers in the fall and the hummingbirds that are attracted to them. In early autumn, the lush, leafy stems terminate with showy tubular flowers, which continue until winter frosts arrive.

TYPE, HABIT, AND SIZE A half-hardy perennial 4–5 feet (1.2–1.5 m) tall and wide.

HARDINESS Zone 9a

ORIGIN Mexico

CULTIVATION Full sun or partial shade in hot, dry climates. Grows best in a good soil with regular water. Pineapple sage is a lush leafy plant that wilts readily when its water needs are not met. It can be cut back in midsummer if the growth is too rank.

LANDSCAPE USE Pineapple sage is easy to place between shrubs or behind groupings of summer-blooming perennials. Then, in early autumn, when much of the garden is quiet, the bright floral display begins.

RELATED PLANTS

'Frieda Dixon' A selection of the species with salmon-pink flowers (see photo on page 35).

'Golden Delicious' A 2012 introduction with bright gold foliage that holds its color through the growing season (see photo on page 18). The combination of gold and scarlet, while not my cup of tea, is very colorful.

Salvia farinacea
Mealy cup sage

Mealy cup sage has been hybridized and used as an annual bedding plant for many years. The plants are tidy and bloom all summer and fall, their vertical stems densely clothed with small flowers that peek from the woolly calyces. The flowering racemes rise above narrow, fresh green leaves. There are many seed strains available with the flower color ranging from dark violet to white. Bees are attracted to the flowers.

TYPE, HABIT, AND SIZE A tender perennial 2 feet (0.6 m) tall and wide.
HARDINESS Zone 9a
ORIGIN New Mexico, Texas, Mexico.
CULTIVATION Easy and adaptable, growing in full sun to light shade. It can get by with little water, but regular irrigation results in more vibrant, floriferous plants. Can overwinter in very mild locations and even self-seed. Deadheading (removing old flowers) increases flower production.
LANDSCAPE USE *Salvia farinacea* cultivars are more popular and more commonly seen in gardens than the species. They are all generally loved as being excellent low-maintenance choices for containers, for the cutting garden, for colorful annual highlights, and for bedding-out. They are also good as dried flower specimens.

RELATED PLANTS
'Blue Bedder' One of the shorter selections at 12 inches (30 cm) tall and wide. Bears flowers of a medium, clear blue.
'Cirrus' Known for its pale pink-lavender, near-white flower spikes with lovely silver gray calyces, stems, and foliage. Grows 18 inches (45 cm) tall and 12 inches (30 cm) wide.
'Evolution' One of the taller cultivars, growing 2–3 feet (69–90 cm) tall and bearing deep violet-blue flowers. An All-America Selections winner for new bedding plants in 2006.
'Raider Azure' A cultivar introduced by Texas Tech in 2008 and pronounced superior in vigor, habit, and overall appearance to other cultivars, particularly in hot, dry locations with lean soil. It grows up to 28 inches (70 cm) tall with an even greater spread and has spikes of dark purple flowers with lighter purple throats.
'Rhea' One of the shorter cultivars, growing 14–16 inches (35–40 cm) tall. It bears intensely blue flowers and bluish calyces, and is noted as one of the earliest bloomers of the strains.
'Victoria' ▶ The most popular of the *S. farinacea* cultivars, this compact perennial forms a nice bushy plant 18–20 inches (45–50 cm) tall and 12 inches (30 cm) wide. Has good green leaves and abundant intensely deep blue-purple flowers on medium spikes from early summer to frost.
'Victoria White' The white flower spikes pair nicely with the fresh green foliage. Grows 24 inches (60 cm) tall.

Salvia flocculosa ▲

This pretty shrub makes a pleasing combination with its glaucous gray-green leaves and plentiful spikes of dark lavender-blue flowers with a wash of white on the lower petals. These are set against the dusky mauve bracts. The open, freely branching shrub produces flowers in summer and fall.

TYPE, HABIT, AND SIZE A tender shrub 4–6 feet (1.2–1.8 m) tall and wide.

HARDINESS Zone 10a

ORIGIN Ecuador

CULTIVATION Do not hesitate to prune and shape as needed to create a strong framework.

LANDSCAPE USE At the San Francisco Botanical Garden (formerly Strybing Arboretum), where tender salvias are grown to perfection, *S. flocculosa* was at one time planted in the Pastel Garden, interplanted with soft pink roses (see photo). It was a beautiful combination. In cold climates, this salvia deserves consideration for mixed container plantings.

Salvia 'Flower Child' ▸

Unique for its beautiful, large lavender-pink flowers, this low-growing, compact salvia has clean foliage and a long floriferous display of flowers from spring through fall.

TYPE, HABIT, AND SIZE A shrubby salvia 18–24 inches (45–60 cm) tall and 18 inches (45 cm) wide.
HARDINESS Zone 8a
ORIGIN One of the cultivars of the *S. greggii/microphylla* complex from Monterey Bay Nursery's Turbulent Sixties series.
CULTIVATION As for all cultivars with this parentage, grow it in full sun to light shade in well-drained soil. Periodically through the growing season, trim the plant back lightly after flushes of flowering.
LANDSCAPE USE An excellent container plant. Use singly or in mass in a variety of landscapes from cottage style and xeric gardens to contemporary (see photo on page 25).

Salvia forsskaolii ▸

A salvia that you never see as a single plant, only as a colony. The basal leaves are large, deep green, hairy, and of differing shapes, creating a generous leafy carpet. The large violet-blue flowers with colorful splashes of white on the lower petals are carried on branched spikes and bloom in mid to late summer.

TYPE, HABIT, AND SIZE A hardy perennial with a basal leaf clump 30 inches (75 cm) wide and with flowering stems to 30 inches (75 cm) tall.
HARDINESS Zone 5
ORIGIN Balkan Peninsula
CULTIVATION An adaptable salvia that will grow in dry conditions, but looks best in good soil with regular irrigation and some afternoon shade. If foliage looks tired in late summer, cut back hard to encourage fresh growth.
LANDSCAPE USE In the light shade of a woodland garden or in a perennial border.

Salvia fruticosa ◄
Greek sage

A variable shrub closely allied to the common garden sage, *S. officinalis*. The hairy leaves are smaller and lobed, grayish green with a distinct silver cast. The plant has an upright habit, and the vertical woody stems can provide an architectural element in flower arrangements. The flowers, in terminal clusters, are light pink.

TYPE, HABIT, AND SIZE An evergreen shrub 30 inches (75 cm) tall and wide.
HARDINESS Zone 9a
ORIGIN Mediterranean
CULTIVATION Full sun and well-drained soil. Quite drought tolerant.
LANDSCAPE USE In herb gardens and dry gardens. Excellent in containers.

Salvia fulgens ►
Cardinal sage

Cardinal sage is impressive with its glistening, brilliant red flowers, set in dusky wine-red calyces. This reasonably sized salvia makes a leafy thicket of slender woody stems. The flowers, with the upper petal covered in silky hairs, open midsummer through fall. Naturally, it is a good plant for hummingbirds.

TYPE, HABIT, AND SIZE A woody perennial 4–5 feet (1.2–1.5 m) tall and 3 feet (0.9 m) wide.
HARDINESS Zone 9a
ORIGIN Mexico
CULTIVATION Good soil amended with compost is required as is regular irrigation in the growing season. Cut back the woody stems nearly to the ground in early spring. Give the plant full sun in cooler climates and partial shade in hot, dry climates. May need the support of other plants or some staking.
LANDSCAPE USE A choice salvia for containers in all climates.

Salvia gesneriiflora
Big Mexican scarlet sage

Big is appropriate in this sage's common name, indicative of the size of the plants, leaves, and flowers. In a mild climate, the plant can grow 8–10 feet (2.4–3.0 m) tall and make an equally wide thicket in one season. It begins flowering late in fall and continues through winter into spring, making it appropriate only for mild climates or greenhouse culture. The flowers are a stunning scarlet held in evenly spaced whorls along the 10-inch (25-cm) inflorescence.

TYPE, HABIT, AND SIZE A semitender shrub 8–10 feet (2.4–3.0 m) tall and 6–8 feet (1.8–2.4 m) wide.

HARDINESS Zone 9a

ORIGIN Mexico, Colombia.

CULTIVATION Good soil and regular water. Thin and cut back woody stems after flowering in late spring.

LANDSCAPE USE Effective for filling a corner space where it has room to grow in all directions.

RELATED PLANTS

'Mountain Form' A more compact selection of the species growing 6–8 feet (1.8–2.4 m) tall and wide. Has bright red flowers and dusky red calyces.

'Tequila' ▲ The most popular form of the species. The stately inflorescence has scarlet flowers highlighted by purple-black calyces. The plant in flower is very striking. The nectar from the flowers, as Ernie Wasson from Cabrillo College shared with me, is very flavorful and tastes different from the straight species.

Salvia glabrescens

For the cool shade garden, *Salvia glabrescens* makes shiny clumps of lettuce green foliage. In late fall the leafy flower stems open with large flowers that range from pink to purple. A long fall is needed for the flowers to be enjoyed.

TYPE, HABIT, AND SIZE A hardy perennial 2 feet (60 cm) tall and wide.
HARDINESS Zone 6a
ORIGIN Japan
CULTIVATION Cool shade is best along with humus-rich soil that does not dry out.
LANDSCAPE USE At home in a woodland garden or shady perennial border.

Salvia glechomaefolia ▸

Ground-ivy sage

A spreading perennial that colonizes an area with short upright stems of midgreen leaves. The small bright blue flowers have white markings that help to light them up in the shade. An easy-to-control little groundcover for partial shade.

TYPE, HABIT, AND SIZE An evergreen, mat-forming perennial 10 inches (25 cm) tall and 5 feet (1.5 m) across.
HARDINESS Zone 9a
ORIGIN Mexico
CULTIVATION Grow in partial shade in good, friable, compost-enhanced soil with moderate water in summer.
LANDSCAPE USE Good for covering a small slope.

Salvia glutinosa ▸

Jupiter's distaff

Not in the top tier of salvias for the garden, Jupiter's distaff is a coarse, leafy plant that spreads by seeding. The large, soft yellow flowers are very pretty, splashed with maroon, and are held well above the foliage. In some parts of the United States, this salvia has the potential for being an invasive plant.

TYPE, HABIT, AND SIZE A hardy perennial 4 feet (1.2 m) tall and 3 feet (0.9 m) wide.
HARDINESS Zone 6a
ORIGIN Europe, Asia
CULTIVATION Grows best in light shade and is tolerant of many soils and irrigation regimes.
LANDSCAPE USE Perennial borders or for covering the ground in partial shade.

Salvia gravida ▾

This salvia is quite elegant when in flower. Tapered clusters of warm fuchsia-colored flowers hang from leafy branches in early winter. Unopened flowers are encased in a green calyx, which in turn is shielded by green bracts flushed with burgundy. Being a tender shrub and winter flowering, this salvia can only be enjoyed in mild, near frost-free climates or as a greenhouse specimen.

TYPE, HABIT, AND SIZE A tender shrub 6 feet (1.8 m) tall and 5 feet (1.5 m) wide.
HARDINESS Zone 10a
ORIGIN Mexico
CULTIVATION Grow in partial shade in good humus-enriched soil. Provide regular water.
LANDSCAPE USE A specimen plant for the shaded mixed border. In the photo, *S. gravida* grows to perfection under canyon live oaks.

Salvia greggii 'Alba' ▾

SYNONYM 'Texas Wedding'

Pure white flowers are freely produced on this shrubby plant. The foliage is bright green. The combination of the bright green leaves and clean white flowers is fresh during the hot summer season.

TYPE, HABIT, AND SIZE A shrubby salvia growing 3 feet (0.9 m) tall and wide.
HARDINESS Zone 7
ORIGIN A selection of a northern Mexican species.
CULTIVATION Grow it in full sun to light shade in soil that drains well. Cut back hard in early spring and trim back lightly periodically during the growing season.
LANDSCAPE USE Stands out best with some shade or planted against a darker green background of shrubs.
RELATED PLANTS
'Furman's Red' Another selection of *S. greggii*, this one a dense upright grower with deep red flowers. Winter hardy. Zone 5b. A Plant Select plant from Denver Botanic Gardens.

Salvia greggii 'Variegata' ▸

SYNONYM 'Desert Blaze'

A variegated salvia with small light green leaves edged in creamy white. It provides a bright background that highlights the scarlet red flowers. A vigorous grower.

TYPE, HABIT, AND SIZE A shrubby salvia growing 2–4 feet (60–120 cm) tall and wide. In mild climates, it will grow to its ultimate size.
HARDINESS Zone 8a
ORIGIN A horticultural selection.
CULTIVATION Grow it in full sun to light shade in soil that drains well. Cut back hard in early spring and trim back lightly periodically during the growing season. Watch and remove any stems that revert to all-green leaves.
LANDSCAPE USE A colorful salvia to use in containers or a perennial border. The leaves are small so the variegation is best appreciated up close.

Salvia guaranitica
Anise-scented sage

Despite the common name, fragrance is not an obvious trait of this sage. What is obvious are the quantities of blue flowers. The richly colored, indigo blue flowers are set against deep green foliage for many months, easily justifying this species as being among the most popular salvias. The growth is strong and leafy. Herbaceous in most zones, the plant begins flowering in early to midsummer and continues well into fall. It can be vigorous in mild climates—even considered invasive—colonizing by interesting, swollen tuberous roots. The species is one of the best salvias for attracting hummingbirds.

TYPE, HABIT, AND SIZE A half-hardy perennial 6 feet (1.8 m) tall and 4–5 feet (1.2–1.5 m) wide.
HARDINESS Zone 8a
ORIGIN Argentina, Brazil, Paraguay, Uruguay.
CULTIVATION Requires regular irrigation and grows best in fertile soils supplemented with compost. In areas with hot summers, some afternoon shade is welcome. The plant begins growth late in the spring, so be patient after a cold winter. Wait to cut the prior season's growth until early spring.
LANDSCAPE USE Easily used in perennial borders as a backdrop for any number of summer-flowering perennials or planted with cannas or coleus for a lush tropical look. It is also substantial enough to plant between shrubs to provide summer color where its vacancy until late-spring emergence will not be missed. Since it grows quickly, this sage is frequently used in cold climates as an annual, blooming through fall until a hard freeze.
RELATED PLANTS
'**Blue Ensign**' Long, elegant spikes of clear, deep blue flowers with light green bracts.
'**Van Remsen**' A tall-growing, nonspreading selection with large rich blue flowers. Late flowering.

Salvia guaranitica 'Argentine Skies'

For some people, 'Argentine Skies' is their favorite *S. guaranitica* selection with its very pale gray-blue flowers. In the California heat, I find it is too pale even in the shade, but in cooler, cloudier climates, the soft blue is more prominent and is quite lovely. 'Argentine Skies' is a very vigorous, strongly upright grower with a generous spreading habit.

TYPE, HABIT, AND SIZE A semihardy perennial 4–6 feet (1.2–1.8 m) tall and 3–6 feet (0.9–1.8 m) wide.
HARDINESS Zone 7
ORIGIN South America
CULTIVATION Provide good soil and plenty of water to sustain the leafy plant, with partial shade in hot sunny climates. Cut to the ground in early spring.
LANDSCAPE USE Easily adapted in the perennial or mixed shrub border, where it can hold its own with other large, vigorous perennials or grasses.

Salvia guaranitica 'Black and Blue'

One of the most popular salvias in the United States, grown for its 5-month display of showy clusters of intense, deep blue flowers set against very dark—near black—calyces. The light green foliage is lush and abundant. Easy and fast growing, this plant is also a favorite of hummingbirds.

TYPE, HABIT, AND SIZE A semihardy perennial 4–6 feet (1.2–1.8 m) tall and 3–5 feet (0.9–1.5 m) wide.
HARDINESS Zone 7
ORIGIN South America
CULTIVATION Needs good soil, plenty of water to sustain the leafy plant, and partial shade in hot sunny climates. Cut to the ground in early spring.
LANDSCAPE USE A perfect plant for a perennial border, complementing a wide array of perennials, either with tall late-summer helianthus, heliopsis, *Rudbeckia nitida* or with the shorter *Rudbeckia* 'Goldsturm.' Large orange or yellow daylilies work well in front. There are many possibilities. It also is very attractive in large containers.

Salvia Heatwave Series

Salvias in the Heatwave series are selections from the *S. greggi/micro-phylla* complex. They tolerate hot, dry conditions and have proven to be very fine garden plants. All are compact growers with long displays of flowers in various colors.

TYPE, HABIT, AND SIZE Shrubby salvias 30 inches (75 cm) tall and 36 inches (90 cm) across.

HARDINESS Zone 7

ORIGIN Horticultural selections from Australia.

CULTIVATION Grow in full sun to light shade in soil that drains well. Cut back hard in early spring and trim back lightly periodically during the growing season. Water deeply and occasionally in the growing season.

LANDSCAPE USE Their long bloom season and compact habit make the Heatwave series suitable as a feature in the dry garden or perennial border planted either singly or in mass.

RELATED PLANTS

Heatwave 'Blast' Coral-pink flowers.

Heatwave 'Blaze' ▲ Rich, saturated red flowers that cover the plant.

Heatwave 'Glimmer' Ivory-white flowers against darker calyces and stems.

Heatwave 'Glitter' Large lavender-pink flowers.

Heatwave 'Sparkle' Bright pink flowers.

Salvia heldreichiana

One of the Mediterranean species that thrives in warm, dry climates, *S. heldreichiana* is an evergreen, semishrubby salvia with grayish green 3-lobed leaves that have a decidedly silver cast. In late spring, the flowering stems rise well above the foliage, creating a cloud of lavender-blue. The large flowers are spaced in whorls along the stem. This salvia is a great attractor of bees, butterflies, and hummingbirds.

TYPE, HABIT, AND SIZE An evergreen shrub 18–24 inches (45–60 cm) tall and 30 inches (75 cm) wide with flowering stems to 3 feet (0.9 m) tall.
HARDINESS Zone 7b
ORIGIN Turkey
CULTIVATION Responds poorly to too much summer water; grow on the dry side in lean soils.
LANDSCAPE USE This salvia fits readily into a Mediterranean garden, large or small. It combines nicely with phlomis, santolina, and the smaller cistus.

Salvia hians

A fine salvia with slightly inflated-looking flowers. The warm violet-blue blossoms are held on many-branched stems that rise above a basal rosette of light green, long, lanceolate leaves.

TYPE, HABIT, AND SIZE A hardy perennial with a clumping habit 2 feet (0.6 m) wide and with flowering stems to 3 feet (0.9 m) tall.

HARDINESS Zone 6a

ORIGIN Pakistan

CULTIVATION Grows best in good soil amended with compost and with regular summer watering. Provide partial shade in hot climates.

LANDSCAPE USE A wonderful salvia to mix with other hardy perennials.

Salvia hierosolymitana

While the pinkish raspberry flowers are intricately beautiful, the foliage alone is reason to grow this salvia. The nicely composed mound of deep green, ribbed leaves with mahogany petioles brings added texture to the landscape.

TYPE, HABIT, AND SIZE A half-hardy evergreen perennial with a clumping growth 30 inches (75 cm) across and with flowering stems to 30 inches (75 cm) tall.

HARDINESS Zone 8b

ORIGIN Mediterranean

CULTIVATION Grows in full sun to light shade in well-drained soils. While it is fairly drought tolerant, it stays fresh and produces more flowers when given regular summer water.

LANDSCAPE USE Could be grown in a partially dryland composition with nepetas, teucriums, and *S. greggii/ microphylla* selections, or in a perennial border.

Salvia 'Honeymelon'

Although this sage is usually listed as a cultivar of *S. elegans*, I have always felt there were enough differences between it and the species that it should be listed as a hybrid. This spreading perennial makes a low, dense mound of fragrant green leaves. In the fall, racemes of evenly spaced scarlet flowers, smaller than those of *S. elegans*, smother the plant. If the winter is not too severe, this sage tends to bloom again through spring.

TYPE, HABIT, AND SIZE A half-hardy perennial 18–24 inches (45–60 cm) tall and 3–4 feet (0.9–1.2 m) wide.
HARDINESS Zone 9a
ORIGIN Introduced by Huntington Botanical Gardens.
CULTIVATION An adaptable salvia that grows in full sun or partial shade. If there is winter damage, cut back the plant nearly to the ground in early spring, otherwise shear it in half after the spring flowering.
LANDSCAPE USE The summertime mounding foliage is attractive through the growing season. It is easy to envision this sage making its dense, leafy mounds in light shade under small trees.
RELATED PLANTS
'Tangerine' Although the fragrance is not as obvious to me as that of 'Honeymelon', the word is that the leaves of this sage smell of tangerine.

Salvia 'Hot Lips'

For good reasons 'Hot Lips' has become a very popular
salvia. It is a vigorous grower with bicolored red-and-white
flowers for 7–9 months of the year. At times, the flowers
can be either all white or all red. In my experience, the
bicolored flowers dominate when the growth is active and
vigorous, before the heat of summer.

TYPE, HABIT, AND SIZE An evergreen shrub 4–5 feet (1.2–
1.5 m) tall and wide.
HARDINESS Zone 8b
ORIGIN A garden in Mexico.
CULTIVATION Grow it in full sun or partial shade. Adaptable to varying amounts of irrigation. Cut back halfway in
early spring when new growth begins from the center of the
plant, and trim as needed to keep neat during the growing
season.
LANDSCAPE USE Use as a colorful accent plant. It is
vigorous and large enough to use as a hedge. Irresistible
to hummingbirds. Does well in a large container.

Salvia 'Indigo Spires'

Long popular with gardeners as a large annual. When
planted in mid or late spring, by late summer 'Indigo Spires'
can be a mass of twisted, waving flowering stems atop
4-foot (1.2-m) tall plants. The flowering stems are long
wands set with small indigo blue flowers clasped in dusky
purple calyces. Flower color deepens with the cooler days
of fall.

TYPE, HABIT, AND SIZE A half-hardy perennial 4–5 feet
(1.2–1.5 m) tall and wide.
HARDINESS Zone 9a
ORIGIN A hybrid of *S. longispicata* and *S. farinacea*.
LANDSCAPE USE Plant in perennial borders for a long
season of color. This salvia is a bit leggy for container
culture unless other plants are grown at its base.

Salvia involucrata

Roseleaf sage

Salvias have an appealing way of using complementary colors and color gradations in the plant as a whole. Roseleaf sage is a branching shrub whose rich green leaves are underlined with reddish veins. The young stems and leaf petioles also pick up these reddish tones, while the vibrant cerise-rose flowers are encased by leafy bracts of the same warm hue. The flowers can begin opening in midsummer and last through fall. This is a very showy species.

TYPE, HABIT, AND SIZE A half-hardy shrub 5–7 feet (1.5–2.1 m) tall and wide.

HARDINESS Zone 9a

ORIGIN Mexico

CULTIVATION Good friable, compost-amended soil with regular watering in summer suits the roseleaf sage. Provide afternoon or partial shade.

LANDSCAPE USE As with many of the larger salvias, roseleaf sage is effective planted with large shrub roses. Its good-looking clean structure is set off nicely when grown against a solid fence or stucco wall. This salvia provides a bright burst of rosy magenta when the fall garden is giving way to autumn tones.

RELATED PLANTS

'Hidalgo' Reputed to be the earliest-flowering selection of the species. A compact grower 4–6 feet (1.2–1.8 m) tall by 3–4 feet (0.9–1.2 m) wide.

'Joan' Has a neat habit and large, open clusters of bright rose-pink flowers. An introduction from Australia thought to be a hybrid with *S. microphylla*.

Salvia ×jamensis 'Golden Girl'

Softly colored, yet not too pale, the flowers are a warm shade of creamy yellow. These are freely produced all season—spring into the fall—over a low-growing plant dense with small, dark green leaves.

TYPE, HABIT, AND SIZE A semievergreen woody subshrub to 2 feet (60 cm) tall and 3 feet (90 cm) across.

HARDINESS Zone 7b

ORIGIN A selection from a cross between *S. greggii* and *S. microphylla*.

CULTIVATION As with all of the cultivars in this complex, it grows in full sun to light shade in well-drained soil. Water deeply periodically during summer.

LANDSCAPE USE A choice plant for container culture where its soft-colored flowers can be appreciated in closer view. Also can be planted in a perennial border.

Salvia jurisicii
Feathered sage

A unique little salvia with very finely cut, dissected foliage that forms a low, light green mat. Most people who see the plant not in flower find it difficult to imagine such foliage belongs to a salvia. Combine the unusual leaves with the upside down (resupinate) frothy flowers and it becomes evident just how varied the world of salvias is. The lavender-blue flowers are closely set, making for a very bright display.

TYPE, HABIT, AND SIZE A hardy perennial forming a low mat 4 inches (10 cm) tall and 18 inches (45 cm) across, with flowering stems to 10 inches (25 cm) tall.
HARDINESS Zone 6a
ORIGIN Balkans
CULTIVATION Grow it in full sun and well-drained soil. While it does not need lots of water, it will stay green in summer if given regular irrigation.
LANDSCAPE USE Good choice for rock gardens, planted among rocks, spilling softly over the edge of a retaining wall, or easing onto a pathway. Can be paired with low-growing dianthus (see photo).
RELATED PLANTS
'Blue' A seed strain of the species that gives rise to plants with dark blue flowers.

Salvia 'Javier'

The softly colored flowers are violet-purple with a pronounced frilly lower lip. These are set off nicely against the pale lime-green foliage.

TYPE, HABIT, AND SIZE A semievergreen subshrub to 2 feet (60 cm) tall and wide.
HARDINESS Zone 7
ORIGIN A hybrid of *Salvia greggii* and *S. microphylla* raised in New Zealand.
CULTIVATION Grow it in full sun to partial shade in well-drained soil.
LANDSCAPE USE As a container plant or in a perennial border.

Salvia koyamae
Japanese yellow sage

Chosen more for its foliage effect in the garden than its flowers, Japanese yellow sage boasts large, pale yellow-green leaves. Each leaf is almost 6 inches (15 cm) long and nearly as wide. The decumbent stems lay on the ground or on nearby plants, creating a soft textural weave through the garden. The flowers, while not showy, are a very pretty soft yellow.

TYPE, HABIT, AND SIZE A half-hardy perennial 2 feet (0.6 m) tall and slowly spreading to 4–6 feet (1.2–1.8 m) across.

HARDINESS Zone 8b

ORIGIN Japan

CULTIVATION Grow in good soil with humus added, regular irrigation, and partial shade. Trim off old flowers to keep the focus on the attractive foliage.

LANDSCAPE USE Plant in a shady perennial border, woodland garden, or the foreground of shrubs.

Salvia lanceolata

Shrubs from South Africa tend to be compact, handsome plants with interesting rather than showy flowers. *Salvia lanceolata* is no different. The leaves are a soft, silver gray and lance-shaped as the species name suggests. The large flowers are variable in color, changing from a muted rose to terra cotta. When the flowers drop, the calyces become a more prominent feature, as they enlarge and deepen to a darker, dusky rose.

TYPE, HABIT, AND SIZE A half-hardy evergreen shrub 3–4 feet (0.9–1.2 m) tall and wide.
HARDINESS Zone 9a
ORIGIN South Africa
CULTIVATION Grow it in full sun in well-drained soil and give occasional summer water. Little pruning is required, but if damage from winter cold occurs, it can be removed in spring.
LANDSCAPE USE Looks quite architectural when planted against a warm-colored stucco or adobe wall.

Salvia lasiantha

Another interesting flower combination. The small flowers, which open midsummer through fall, are a soft apricot set inside hairy, rosy mauve bracts—a subtle, soft blending of colors. The leaves have a fine pebbly texture and are narrow and pointed. Altogether, this salvia makes an attractive upright-flowering shrub.

TYPE, HABIT, AND SIZE A half-hardy shrub 5–7 feet (1.5–2.1 m) tall and 4 feet (1.2 m) wide.
HARDINESS Zone 9a
ORIGIN Central America
CULTIVATION Grow in partial shade in humus-enriched soil and provide regular water. In mild climates, thin out older stems in spring to encourage new growth.
LANDSCAPE USE This sage has a subtle effect in the landscape so plant it close in—up against the house or a wall.

Salvia lavandulifolia
Spanish sage

For the hot, dry garden, Spanish sage is a perfect fit. It makes a low-growing woody shrublet set with linear silvery gray leaves. In late spring, the masses of lavender-blue flowers rise well above the foliage on slender stems. The leaves are strongly scented.

TYPE, HABIT, AND SIZE An evergreen shrublet with foliage 4–12 inches (10–30 cm) tall and 2–3 feet (60–90 cm) wide and with flowering stems to 15 inches (38 cm) tall.
HARDINESS Zone 8b
ORIGIN Spain, France.
CULTIVATION Needs good drainage, lean soil, and limited water.
LANDSCAPE USE In the xeric landscape, Spanish sage combines readily with eriogonum, penstemon, and other dryland perennials. It is also fitting to use in an herb garden, as it is a popular cooking herb in Spain.

Salvia lavanduloides

Lavender-like is the rationale for the species name and evidently so. The lavender-blue flowers are arranged tightly at the tip of erect flowering stems. The plant is not spectacular or particularly showy, but still an attractive salvia when in flower.

TYPE, HABIT, AND SIZE A half-hardy shrub 30 inches (75 cm) tall and wide.
HARDINESS Zone 9a
ORIGIN Central America
CULTIVATION Grow in partial shade, especially in hotter climates. Needs well-drained soil and moderate summer water.
LANDSCAPE USE Well suited for containers.

Salvia leucantha
Mexican bush sage

Mexican bush sage may be the most widely planted salvia in California. Seeing it in full bloom—in all its velvety floriferous glory, busy with hungry hummingbirds—makes it easy to understand its popularity. In cooler, mild climates, it blooms summer through fall, while in hotter zones it grows through summer, then blooms all fall. The plant makes a thicket of stems set with lance-shaped leaves that are grayish green on top and fuzzy white underneath. The inflorescence rises well above the foliage and consists of small, tubular, white flowers that extend from fuzzy purple calyces. What a contrast! Outstanding as a cut flower.

TYPE, HABIT, AND SIZE A half-hardy perennial 4–6 feet (1.2–1.8 m) tall and wide.
HARDINESS Zone 8a
ORIGIN Mexico
CULTIVATION While tolerant of many soils, it requires good drainage, particularly in winter. Grow it in full sun. This very drought tolerant salvia tends to become lanky with too much water and then requires staking. Cut old foliage to the ground in early spring.
LANDSCAPE USE Mexican bush sage stands well on its own in the landscape. When it is in its full glory of bloom, being surrounded perhaps by the season-ending foliage of grasses or the simple rounded shapes of shrubs is enough. It can be grown on a sunny bank (see photo) as well as for cut flowers.
RELATED PLANTS
'Midnight' The flowers are deep violet nearly matching the calyces.
'Santa Barbara' A compact cultivar growing 30 inches (75 cm) tall. Flower color is similar to 'Midnight' but slightly lighter. An excellent salvia.

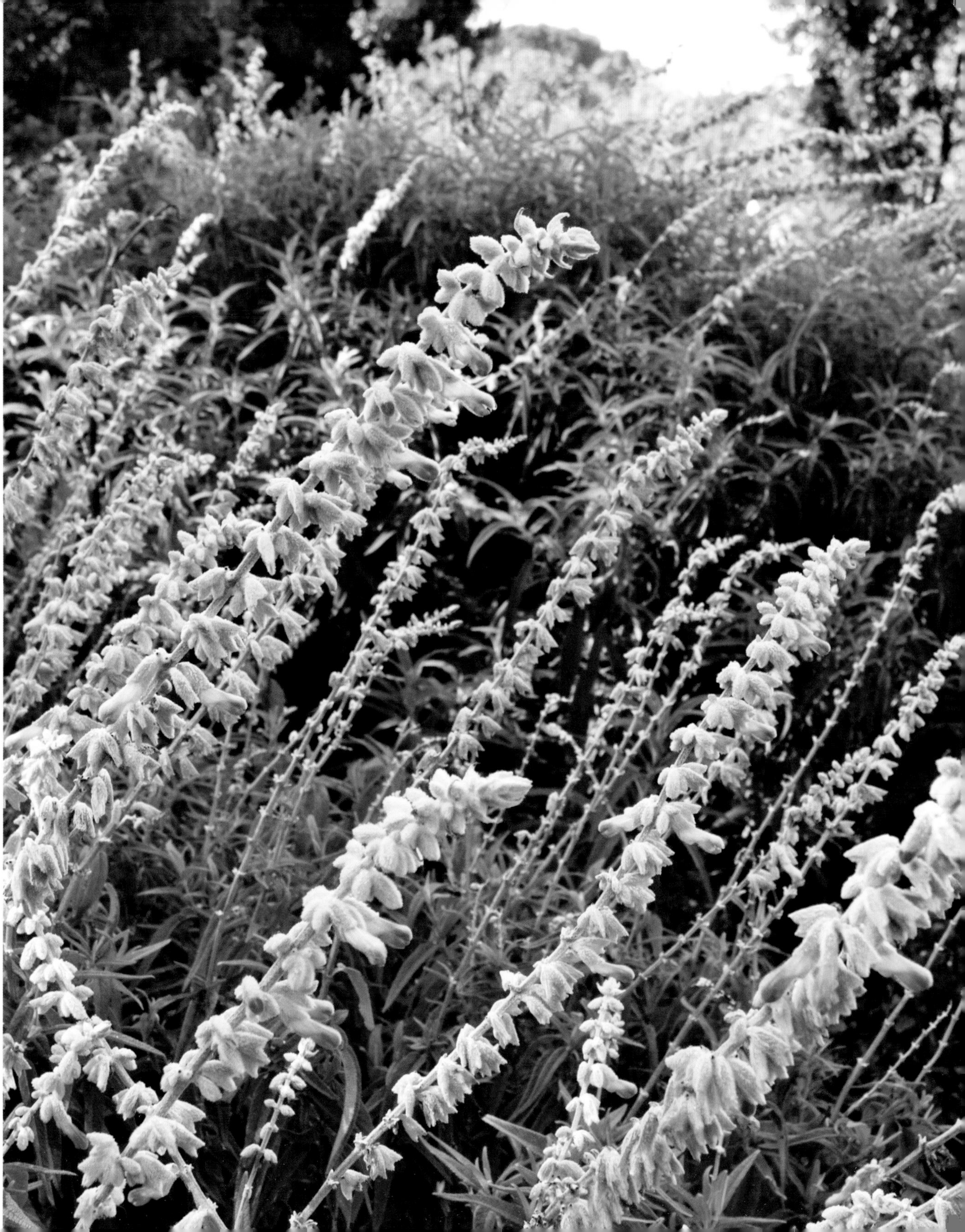

Salvia leucantha 'Velour Pink'◄

Similar in all ways to the species except, in this selection, warm pink flowers emerge from fuzzy, silvery white calyces. The combination is very pretty.

TYPE, HABIT, AND SIZE A half-hardy perennial to 4 feet (1.2 m) tall and wide.
HARDINESS Zone 8a
ORIGIN An Australian selection of a Mexican species.
CULTIVATION Tolerant of many soils, but good drainage is important, particularly in winter. Grow it in full sun. Although it is quite drought tolerant, it tends to become lanky with too much water and then requires staking. Cut old foliage to the ground in early spring.
LANDSCAPE USE Like the species, this selection stands well on its own.
RELATED PLANTS
'Velour White' An all-white selection of the species.

Salvia leucophylla▲
Purple sage

A native sage that has found a home in many California gardens because it is tough, good-looking year-round and endures heat, drought, and poor soils. It has a mounding, spreading habit of silver foliage. The narrow leaves are textured and scented, of course. The flowers, light rose to lavender-pink in tightly stacked whorls, are attractive to bumblebees and honeybees.

TYPE, HABIT, AND SIZE A semievergreen shrub with mounding growth 4–6 feet (1.2–1.8 m) tall and 5–15 feet (1.5–4.5 m) across.
HARDINESS Zone 8b
ORIGIN California
CULTIVATION Grow it in full sun in well-drained soil. Little water is required to keep this plant healthy looking.
LANDSCAPE USE Makes a large silver foliage accent in the dry, native plant garden. Excellent for covering ground in exposed conditions. Can be used to soften rocks by a pool, as in the photo where *Teucrium cossonii* (syn. *T. majoricum*) grows at its feet.
RELATED PLANTS
'Amethyst Bluff' Selected for its deeper colored rosy pink flowers, this large grower reaches 6 feet (1.8 m) tall and spreads to 10–15 feet (3.0–4.5 m) across.
'Pinkie' Selected for its deeper pink flowers.
'Point Sal Spreader' Growing 30 inches (75 cm) tall and to 10 feet (3 m) across, this selection is well suited as a groundcover or erosion control on banks.

Salvia lycioides ▸
Canyon sage

Small slender branches arise from a woody base. The small, midgreen leaves are sparse as are the small bright blue flowers. Canyon sage is not a showy plant, rather one that maintains a simple, natural appearance.

TYPE, HABIT, AND SIZE A hardy perennial or subshrub 12 inches (30 cm) tall and 24 inches (60 cm) wide.
HARDINESS Zone 7b
ORIGIN Texas, New Mexico, Mexico.
CULTIVATION Grow it in full sun to light shade in well-drained soil. Little summer water is required.
LANDSCAPE USE Plant in a rock garden among plants that do not overshadow its delicate habit.

Salvia macrophylla

Big leaves, lush and fast growing, and with some of the truest blue flowers in the salvia world make this a desirable salvia. The leaves are sticky and hairy and can be as long as 12 inches (30 cm). The branched inflorescence carries the large blue flowers from midsummer through fall.

TYPE, HABIT, AND SIZE A tender perennial 6 feet (1.8 m) tall and 5 feet (1.5 m) wide.
HARDINESS Zone 10a
ORIGIN South America
CULTIVATION Grow in partial shade in rich soil and provide plenty of water.
LANDSCAPE USE Can be planted in the ground or in containers, wherever a bold lush look is wanted. Its fast growth makes it a good candidate to grow for summertime foliage and flowers in colder zones.
RELATED PLANTS
'Purple Leaf' ▸ The purple underside of these generous leaves gives a whole new look and a decidedly more exotic, tropical look than the plain-green species.

Salvia madrensis▾

Forsythia sage

You can practically watch some salvias growing and this is one of them. Once forsythia sage begins its growth when the soil warms, the large angular square stems, set with large heart-shaped leaves, seem to shoot up inches a day. By late summer, the strong, vertical stems have made a handsome lush plant. In early fall, the nearly foot-long (30-cm) inflorescence opens with warm yellow flowers.

TYPE, HABIT, AND SIZE A half-hardy perennial 5–7 feet (1.5–2.1 m) tall and 5 feet (1.5 m) wide.
HARDINESS Zone 9a
ORIGIN Mexico
CULTIVATION Grow in partial shade in compost-enhanced soil, and water regularly in the growing season. Cut to the ground in early spring.
LANDSCAPE USE Makes a bright complementary combination when planted with other late-season salvias such the selections of *S. mexicana* or with blue-flowered *S.* 'Costa Rican Blue' (see photo).

Salvia madrensis 'Red Neck Girl'

Red-stemmed forsythia sage

Stems are rarely an advertised feature of a plant, but in 'Red Neck Girl' the already dramatic square stems of *S. madrensis*, which can be nearly 2 inches (5 cm) in diameter, are a deep maroon red acting as a vertical accent running up through the large bold leaves. An eye-catching plant for foliage and form.

TYPE, HABIT, AND SIZE A tender perennial with a strongly upright habit to 5–7 feet (1.5–2.1 m) tall and slowly spreading to 4 feet (1.2 m) across.

HARDINESS Zone 9a

ORIGIN Mexico

CULTIVATION Grow in partial shade and good compost-enhanced soil. Provide regular watering in the growing season. The species is a fast grower when conditions are right and looks best if not deprived of water or partial shade. Cut to the ground in early spring.

LANDSCAPE USE Despite being tender, it is fast growing so can be used to good effect in all climates, whether in a large container or in a border where a bold tropical look is desired.

Salvia 'Marine Blue'

It is unclear whether 'Marine Blue' is a sport or a hybrid of *S. chamaedryoides*. Whatever its origin, it is a very nice cultivar and essentially an enhanced version of the species. The gray leaves are slightly larger than those of *S. chamaedryoides*, as are the deep indigo blue flowers. Like *S. chamaedryoides*, it also spreads slowly underground, gradually increasing its spread.

TYPE, HABIT, AND SIZE A shrubby perennial 2 feet (0.6 m) tall and 4 feet (1.2 m) wide.
HARDINESS Zone 9a
ORIGIN May be a sport or a hybrid of *S. chamaedryoides*.
CULTIVATION Grow in full sun to light shade in well-drained soil. Provide occasional water in the growing season. Shear as needed to maintain a denser habit.
LANDSCAPE USE In perennial borders, larger rock gardens, along pathways, and in containers.

Salvia melissodora
Grape-scented sage

One of only a few salvias whose flowers have a distinct fragrance. In this case, the small lavender flowers in short racemes have a sweet smell of grape, as the plant's common name suggests. The scent is evident when walking past the plant on a still, warm day. The small, textured leaves are slightly hairy. From early fall through winter, the flowers of this attractive-looking woody shrub entice many bees and butterflies.

TYPE, HABIT, AND SIZE A semideciduous shrub 6–8 feet (1.8–2.4 m) tall and 4–6 feet (1.2–1.8 m) wide.
HARDINESS Zone 9a
ORIGIN Mexico
CULTIVATION Grow it in full sun to light shade in well-drained soil. Although fairly drought tolerant, grape-scented sage also can accept more frequent watering. Prune and thin out woody branches in late spring or fall to maintain shape.
LANDSCAPE USE Planted against a warm south-facing wall protects it and encourages a long blooming season. Would be suitable to trim as an espalier.

Salvia mellifera
Black sage

Black sage is a dominant plant in the California coastal scrub community. This salvia is also considered, as the species name suggests, highly attractive to bees (*Apis mellifera* is the scientific name for honeybees). The wrinkled, narrow leaves are strongly fragrant. The flowers in whorls range from near white to pale blue.

TYPE, HABIT, AND SIZE An evergreen shrub 4 feet (1.2 m) tall and wide.

HARDINESS Zone 9a

ORIGIN California

CULTIVATION Extremely drought tolerant, black sage does best in full sun in well-drained soil. Prune in early spring or early fall to shape the plant.

LANDSCAPE USE The flowers are not particularly showy, but the dark olive green foliage provides some contrast in the xeric, native plant landscape.

RELATED PLANTS

'Dara's Choice' A hybrid with blue flowers in late spring and early summer.

'Green Carpet' A low-mounding selection with midblue flowers. Grows 2 feet (0.6 m) tall and 4 feet (1.2 m) wide. An easy-to-use cultivar for the small dry garden.

'Mrs. Beard' A hybrid with blue flowers in late spring and early summer.

'Terra Seca' A low-growing selection 2 feet (0.6 m) tall and spreading to 6–8 feet (1.8–2.4 m). An excellent plant for covering hot exposed sites.

Salvia 'Mesa Azure' ▲

Often sold as a selection of *S. greggii*, but clearly a plant of mixed parentage. 'Mesa Azure' has a woody habit with a good balance of foliage and flowers. While it does not produce masses of flowers, it is always in bloom with short wiry stems sprinkled above the dark green foliage holding open pairs of flowers. It is one of my favorite small shrubby salvias.

TYPE, HABIT, AND SIZE A small, evergreen, semideciduous shrub 18–24 inches (45–60 cm) tall and to 30 inches (75 cm) wide.

HARDINESS Zone 7

ORIGIN A horticultural selection of species from Texas and northern Mexico.

CULTIVATION Grow it in full sun to light shade in well-drained soil. After first flowering, cut back if you desire a more compact plant and halfway in early spring. I do not mind the woody nature of 'Mesa Azure'.

LANDSCAPE USE 'Mesa Azure' has a natural look to it and would be at home among rocks, small grasses, small silver artemisias, yellow buckwheats, or erigerons. It also makes an attractive container plant.

RELATED PLANTS

There are several other color selections of the Mesa series: **'Mesa Scarlet'**, **'Mesa Rose'**, and **'Mesa Purple'**.

Salvia mexicana 'Limelight' ▲

This selection of Mexican bush sage is notable when in late summer the beautiful combination of chartreuse calyces and deep blue flowers opens on large elongated spikes. These will bloom long into the fall until the first hard freeze.

TYPE, HABIT, AND SIZE A half-hardy shrub 5–8 feet (1.5–2.4 m) tall and 4–6 feet (1.2–1.8 m) wide.
HARDINESS Zone 8a
ORIGIN Mexico
CULTIVATION Grow in partial shade in well-drained soil amended with compost. The plants need water, but as with some of the salvias, too much water encourages rank growth. Branches are brittle, so cut back some of the lankier stems during the growing season. Do major pruning in spring.
LANDSCAPE USE Effective when planted with other large salvias, particularly *S. madrensis*, but also can be used in the back of a mixed border, rising above lower shrubs and perennials, bringing some mellow color to the fall garden.
RELATED PLANTS
'Ocampo' Near black calyces with purple-blue flowers make this selection of the species quite striking.

Salvia microphylla var. *neurepia* ▲

A robust plant with large (for a *S. microphylla*) substantial leaves and vigorous growth that is topped by short stalks of deep red flowers. This variety of the species is of a much different scale than others in this group and is a favorite of bumblebees and hummingbirds. There is always activity in its midst.

TYPE, HABIT, AND SIZE A semievergreen woody subshrub 4–5 feet (1.2–1.5 m) tall and wide.
HARDINESS Zone 7a
ORIGIN Mexico
CULTIVATION Grows in full sun to light shade and is quite drought tolerant, but looks fresher with occasional deep watering in the summer. Shear off spent flowers after the first flush of spring blooms and prune hard (cut back halfway) in early spring.
LANDSCAPE USE This salvia is large enough to hold its own with large shrubs. Mine with *Rosa mutabilis* on an infrequently irrigated hillside is a durable and pleasing combination. Big enough to use as a hedge and helps keep deer away from the rose.

Salvia microphylla 'San Carlos Festival'

A very dependable and attractive shrubby salvia that achieves a good balance between foliage and flowers. Unlike most of the shrubby *S. greggii/microphylla* selections whose leaves are not a feature, this has arrow-shaped, olive green leaves, slightly rugose, that clothe the stems densely. Short stems carry the magenta-pink flowers just above the foliage, tending to be produced in periodic spurts during the growing season.

TYPE, HABIT, AND SIZE A shrubby salvia 18–30 inches (45–75 cm) tall and to 30 inches (75 cm) wide.
HARDINESS Zone 7
ORIGIN Mexico
CULTIVATION Grow it in full sun to light shade in soil that drains well. Cut back hard in early spring and trim back lightly during the growing season.
LANDSCAPE USE Because of its dense foliage and compact nature, 'San Carlos Festival' can be used as a small hedge, as I have done in my small front garden, to separate informal lawn from mixed plantings. Very nice in containers.

Salvia muirii ▲

This is a cute little shrub that, if only it were a tad hardier, would be seen in more gardens. The leaves are small, at less than 1 inch (2.5 cm) long, and like those of other South African shrubs have some substance to them. The flowers are relatively large compared to the leaves and are quite showy—a beautiful midblue with a bright splash of white.

TYPE, HABIT, AND SIZE A half-hardy subshrub 1 foot (30 cm) tall and 2 feet (60 cm) wide.
HARDINESS Zone 9a
ORIGIN South Africa
CULTIVATION Grow it in full sun to light shade in well-drained soil and give occasional irrigation.
LANDSCAPE USE Perfect for a small rock garden in a mild climate. An easy specimen for growing in a container.

Salvia 'Mulberry Jam' ▶

Selected by salvia expert Betsy Clebsch, 'Mulberry Jam' has long been a favorite of mine. I like its upright, slender habit, which usually arches out as if looking for sunlight. The fuzzy flowers are a clear, hot pink, warmed by the more deeply colored calyces. These flowers can be seen from a distance, but are never gaudy, just bright and cheerful.

TYPE, HABIT, AND SIZE A half-hardy perennial 4 feet (1.2 m) tall and 3 feet (0.9 m) wide.
HARDINESS Zone 9a
ORIGIN A seedling of *S. involucrata* discovered in Betsy Clebsch's garden.
CULTIVATION Grow it in full sun or partial shade in hotter climates. Does best in good soil that is well drained. Prune back hard after winter and trim any lanky branches during the growing season.
LANDSCAPE USE It is not difficult to find a place for this late-summer and fall-blooming salvia. With legs that are best seen from the knees up, 'Mulberry Jam' can be tucked in among roses, in a perennial garden with fall-blooming asters, or rising up behind low shrubs, such as boxwood or hebe.

Salvia 'Mystic Spires Blue'

'Mystic Spires Blue' is more compact than its parent,
S. 'Indigo Spires'. The shiny, deep green foliage makes
a mound less than 1 foot (30 cm) tall. Rising above this
mound are the 12- to 18-inch (30- to 45-cm) long
flowering stems, set with dark purple-blue flowers in
violet-purple calyces. The color combination is very rich
and showy. The flowers bloom from late spring through
fall and are highly attractive to bees of all sorts.

TYPE, HABIT, AND SIZE A half-hardy perennial 30 inches
(75 cm) tall and 2 feet (0.6 m) wide.
HARDINESS Zone 8b
ORIGIN A horticultural selection from S. 'Indigo Spires'.
CULTIVATION Easy to grow in full sun to light shade in good,
well-drained soil. Can endure dry conditions but looks best
with regular watering.
LANDSCAPE USE A perfect salvia to use in mass plantings,
where it provides a long season of bloom. May be tucked in
a mixed border and is a good choice for container culture.

Salvia namaensis

Nama sage

Many plants used in the dry garden have gray-green or silvery gray leaves, but Nama sage (named for the region in South Africa where it is native) is an exception. With its dark green feathery foliage, it provides contrast and a fresh green look in the xeric landscape. The light blue flowers, while attractive, are secondary to the foliage color and form, as they are relatively small and nestled among the dense foliage. The foliage is sticky and has a pleasant fragrance that is spicy with cedar overtones.

TYPE, HABIT, AND SIZE A half-hardy, woody perennial or shrub 3–4 feet (0.9–1.2 m) tall and 3–5 feet (0.9–1.5 m) wide.
HARDINESS Zone 9a
ORIGIN South Africa
CULTIVATION Nama sage is a tough plant, surviving just fine in hot, sunny exposures with little water. It can sprout from the base after a cold winter.
LANDSCAPE USE It seems natural to grow this sage with lavender, cistus, phlomis, eriogonum, and other plants adapted to a Mediterranean climate. A gardener friend has planted a row of Nama sage along her property line in an area with no irrigation. Her intention is to shear it into a casual hedge.

Salvia nana

This is a striking plant for foliage and flowers. The 3-inch (7.5-cm) long dark green leaves with a hint of purple have a pronounced pebbled texture. Tight clusters of rich blue flowers stand out against the dark low mat of foliage.

TYPE, HABIT, AND SIZE A tender perennial 6 inches (15 cm) tall and 12–18 inches (30–45 cm) across.
HARDINESS Zone 9b
ORIGIN Central America
CULTIVATION Grow in partial shade in most climates and water regularly.
LANDSCAPE USE Excellent for container plantings, either by itself or in mixed plantings where it provides great textural contrast with smaller-leaved plants.
RELATED PLANTS
'Curling Waves' A European selection of the species, with flowers produced on taller stems rising well above the foliage.

Salvia 'Nazareth'

Quite a nice salvia, making a dense, full plant of narrow, very silvery white leaves topped in spring with softly colored lavender-blue flowers. A beautiful plant grown primarily for the silver foliage, which is distinctively aromatic, but also for the pretty display of flowers that attract a wide range of pollinators. Closely related to the culinary sage.

TYPE, HABIT, AND SIZE An evergreen shrub 30 inches (75 cm) tall and 36 inches (90 cm) wide.
HARDINESS Zone 6
ORIGIN Mediterranean
CULTIVATION Very tough and drought tolerant, it resents too much water. Grow it in full sun in well-drained soil. Shear spent flowers to highlight the foliage.
LANDSCAPE USE Highly effective for providing a strong silvery accent in the garden, whether a larger rock garden, herb garden, or xeric garden.

Salvia nipponica

A fine sage for the shade garden. The light green leaves are slightly hairy and triangular. Very pretty soft yellow flowers open on flowering stalks set well above the foliage in late summer to early fall.

TYPE, HABIT, AND SIZE A hardy perennial forming a mound of foliage 12 inches (30 cm) tall and 18 inches (45 cm) wide with flowering stems to 18 inches (45 cm) tall.

HARDINESS Zone 6a

ORIGIN Japan

CULTIVATION Grow in partial to full shade, depending on the climate, and provide moist yet well-drained soil.

LANDSCAPE USE Use in the woodland garden or shady perennial border.

RELATED PLANTS
'Fuji Snow' A selection of the species with arrowhead-shaped leaves bordered in creamy white. The variegation is quite striking early in the season.

Salvia nubicola ▸

Another hardy salvia that thrives in a partially shaded border or woodland garden. A handsome leafy plant with large arrowhead-shaped leaves. In late summer the large yellow flowers, with maroon touches, are carried in spikes just above the foliage.

TYPE, HABIT, AND SIZE A hardy perennial 3–4 feet (0.9–1.2 m) tall and wide.

HARDINESS Zone 6b

ORIGIN Central Asia

CULTIVATION Grow it in full to partial shade in compost-enhanced soil with adequate moisture.

LANDSCAPE USE This salvia provides a strong foliage element in a woodland garden (see photo) or partially shaded perennial border. It would partner well with lavender to purple asters in late summer and fall.

Salvia officinalis
Garden sage

This sage could be considered the signature plant representing the genus *Salvia*. It has been grown for centuries and is still popular today. It has a mounding habit of oval gray-green leaves that are, of course, fragrant when rubbed, and it produces many spikes of lavender-blue flowers in midspring. Garden sage is a necessary plant for every herb garden with a variety of foliage choices available.

TYPE, HABIT, AND SIZE A hardy evergreen perennial or shrub with a mounding habit 18 inches (45 cm) tall and 24–30 inches (60–75 cm) wide.

HARDINESS Zone 5

ORIGIN Mediterranean

CULTIVATION Grow it in full sun in average soil that drains well. Is fairly drought tolerant.

LANDSCAPE USE Herb gardens, cottage gardens, edging pathways.

RELATED PLANTS

'Berggarten' Selected for its large gray leaves. Has few flowers.

'Compacta' or **'Minima'** Grows to 10 inches (25 cm) tall and spreads to 18 inches (45 cm) across. Has narrower leaves.

'Icterina' The leaves are broadly edged in creamy gold (see photo on page 21).

'Purpurescens' New leaves are dusky purple, giving a distinct purple cast to the plant (see photo on page 20).

'Tricolor' ▲ Loved for its kaleidoscope of colors. The green leaves have a generous margin of creamy white and the new leaves are flushed with pink.

Salvia oxyphora
Bolivian sage

A very showy species with stunning orange-red flowers that are covered in hairs and are sweetly scented. The plant is luxuriant with large, lanceolate leaves that clothe the upright stems.

TYPE, HABIT, AND SIZE A half-hardy, upright-growing perennial that spreads underground and grows to 4–6 feet (1.2–1.8 m) tall and 3–4 feet (0.9–1.2 m) wide.
HARDINESS Zone 8b with protection
ORIGIN Bolivia
CULTIVATION Does best in rich, well-drained soil with plenty of water in partial shade. Give more shade in hotter climates and more sun in cooler climates. The plant may get lanky when grown in too much shade.
LANDSCAPE USE An excellent choice for containers in all climates where it should bloom from midsummer through fall.

Salvia pachyphylla
Rose sage

This amazing salvia combines intense fragrant foliage with intensely colored flowers. It makes a low-mounding plant of slightly cupped, silvery gray leaves. In midsummer spectacular inflorescences of tubular pink flowers stretch beyond the rosy pink bracts, while the long stamens add drama to the scene.

TYPE, HABIT, AND SIZE A hardy evergreen shrub 2–3 feet (60–90 cm) tall and wide.

HARDINESS Zone 5

ORIGIN California, Nevada, Arizona.

CULTIVATION A rugged salvia that performs best in arid climates such as New Mexico, Colorado, and higher elevations of California. In other climates it may be short-lived. Needs excellent drainage.

LANDSCAPE USE Very much a plant for the xeric landscape, blending naturally with agastache, eriogonum, penstemon, and nepeta.

Salvia patens
Gentian sage

Gentian sage is one of those plants where you cannot help but pause at its showy beauty, and also the simplicity of its flowers. The true species has blue flowers as do most cultivars, but there are forms with bicolored, lavender, and white flowers as well. All are easy, long-blooming salvias.

TYPE, HABIT, AND SIZE A half-hardy perennial ranging in height, depending on the cultivar, 16–48 inches (40–120 cm) tall.
HARDINESS Zone 9a
ORIGIN Mexico
CULTIVATION Prefers a site in partial shade with compost-enriched soil that drains well. Give regular irrigation during the growing season. The plant has a tuberous root, which is easily dug up in fall and potted up to carry the plant through winter in a cool greenhouse, sunroom, or garage.
LANDSCAPE USE Because the flowers are loosely arranged, they are best seen and enjoyed without too much busyness around them. The shorter forms can be planted in front of green shrubs, while the larger-growing varieties planted behind. Container culture enables close inspection of the flowers. The taller varieties may need staking.
RELATED PLANTS
'Cambridge Blue' Large sky blue flowers.
'Dot's Delight' ▲ Sky blue flowers with white on the lower petal. Very striking.
'Lavender Lady' Richly colored large lavender flowers. Grows 2 feet (0.6 m) tall.
'White Trophy' Pure white flowers.

Salvia patens 'Guanajuato'

Spectacular is an easy word to describe this selection of *S. patens*. It produces a multitude of immense, true blue flowers on slender upright stems. The foliage is dark green with darker markings in the center. When in bloom, this large plant looks from a distance like a bevy of blue butterflies.

TYPE, HABIT, AND SIZE A half-hardy perennial that makes loose upright growth 3–5 feet (0.9–1.5 m) tall and to 3 feet (0.9 m) across.
HARDINESS Zone 8b with protection.
ORIGIN Mexico
CULTIVATION Prefers partial shade with good compost-enriched soil that drains well. Give regular irrigation during the growing season. The tuberous roots make the plant easy to dig up in fall; pot up the roots and carry them through winter in a cool greenhouse, sunroom, or garage.
LANDSCAPE USE Because the flowers are loosely arranged, they are best seen and enjoyed without too much busyness around them. Plant it behind green shrubs. May need staking.

Salvia 'Phyllis' Fancy'

Similar to S. 'Waverly', 'Phyllis' Fancy' has crisp, deep green foliage and a subtle flower color. The plant sends up strong stems that arch outward through the season, making a tall, full, fountain-shaped salvia. In late summer through fall, the floral racemes unfurl. The fuzzy, tubular flowers are white, flushed with pale lavender-pink, combining beautifully with the richer lavender calyces.

TYPE, HABIT, AND SIZE A half-hardy perennial 5–7 feet (1.5–2.1 m) tall and 5–8 feet (1.5–2.4 m) wide.

HARDINESS Zone 9a

ORIGIN A seedling discovered in the University of California Santa Cruz garden.

CULTIVATION This hybrid appreciates regular irrigation and a decent soil amended with compost. It will grow in full sun to partial shade in hot climates. Cut it to the ground in early spring.

LANDSCAPE USE Place 'Phyllis' Fancy' behind smaller shrubs or perennials where it will provide color from midsummer to fall. It blends beautifully with late asters, helianthus, and tall grasses such as miscanthus.

RELATED PLANTS

'Meigan's Magic' From Australia, this hybrid is similar to 'Phyllis' Fancy', only with a stronger contrast between flower and bract. The flowers are near white and the bracts are inky blue.

Salvia pisidica▸

A low-growing hardy salvia well suited for the rock garden. The 6-inch (15-cm) stems of bright violet-blue and white-striped flowers smother the fragrant silvery mats in early summer. This is a pleasing little salvia.

TYPE, HABIT, AND SIZE A hardy perennial 4 inches (10 cm) tall and 30 inches (75 cm) across.
HARDINESS Zone 6
ORIGIN Turkey
CULTIVATION Needs sharp drainage and full sun.
LANDSCAPE USE Rock gardens, edging pathways, softening retaining walls.

Salvia pomifera▸

A rugged, drought-tolerant salvia that makes an attractive rounded shrub of narrow, wavy-margined, silvery gray leaves that are highly aromatic. The medium-sized flowers are lavender-blue set in bright rose-colored calyces. This combination makes the inflorescence quite conspicuous.

TYPE, HABIT, AND SIZE An evergreen shrub to 3 feet (90 cm) tall and 3–4 feet (90–120 cm) wide.
HARDINESS Zone 8b
ORIGIN Greece
CULTIVATION Well-drained soil and little summer water are the main considerations when placing this salvia in the garden. Avoid overhead water in the summer months. A site in full sun on a slope would be ideal.
LANDSCAPE USE A natural companion to other very drought tolerant plants such as rosemary, cistus, phlomis, and many of the California native sages.

Salvia pratensis

Meadow clary

From a clump of rough leaves, quantities of large hooded flowers arise. In the species, the flower color would be blue, but there are now many cultivars with pink, rose, or bicolored flowers. All are very showy and elegant when in flower.

TYPE, HABIT, AND SIZE A hardy herbaceous perennial 18–36 inches (45–90 cm) tall and 12–18 inches (30–45 cm) across, depending on the cultivar.

HARDINESS Zone 4

ORIGIN Eurasia

CULTIVATION Easily grown in full sun to light shade with regular water. The species and selections are cold-tolerant, rugged plants that live longer when grown in well-draining soil. Remove the old flowers to encourage reblooming.

LANDSCAPE USE The meadow clary works well in perennial borders or lightly shaded woodland gardens. The species and its selections are good bee and butterfly plants.

RELATED PLANTS

'Indigo' Deep violet-blue flowers growing 24–30 inches (60–75 cm) tall.

'Madeline' A bicolor with blue-and-white flowers.

'Pink Delight' ▲ Deep rose-pink flowers on short 12- to 18-inch (30- to 45-cm) stems.

'Swan Lake' A pure white selection.

'Twilight Serenade' Showy violet-blue flowers on 20-inch (50-cm) stems.

Salvia przewalskii

Handsome mounds of large, lush yellow-green leaves are a feature of this perennial salvia. The flowers, which open in summer, are a dark lavender-purple. While not produced in quantities, they add to the subtle beauty of the plant.

TYPE, HABIT, AND SIZE A hardy perennial forming a mound of foliage 2 feet (0.6 m) tall and 3 feet (0.9 m) wide.
HARDINESS Zone 6
ORIGIN China
CULTIVATION Grow it in full sun to partial shade in good soil and provide regular water.
LANDSCAPE USE An adaptable plant for a perennial border where the foliage will provide textural contrast.

Salvia puberula◄

Hairy roseleaf sage

This salvia is a very attractive perennial or shrub under the light shade of trees where it makes an open woody plant clothed with substantial heart-shaped leaves. In the fall, each stem is topped by short clusters of magenta-pink flowers. The plant is very showy when in bloom and is closely related to *S. involucrata*.

TYPE, HABIT, AND SIZE A half-hardy perennial or shrub 4 feet (1.2 m) tall and wide.
HARDINESS Zone 9a
ORIGIN Mexico
CULTIVATION Grow it in full to partial shade in compost-enriched soil and water regularly.
LANDSCAPE USE A good understory plant in a woodland garden and shady perennial border. Because it is fast growing, it is suitable for use as an annual.

Salvia puberula 'El Butano'◄

Dense clusters of magenta-pink flowers top the leafy stems from fall through winter in mild climates. Collected at 7000 feet (2100 m) in Nuevo Léon (state), Mexico, it is a relatively hardy selection. As with all the *S. puberula*/*S. involucrata* selections, this is a favorite of hummingbirds.

TYPE, HABIT, AND SIZE A half-hardy shrub or perennial, with open growth 4–6 feet (1.2–1.8 m) tall and wide.
HARDINESS Zone 8
ORIGIN Central Mexico
CULTIVATION Grows best in partial shade in well-drained, compost-enhanced soil. Provide regular water in the growing season. Cut back in midsummer if a more compact plant is desired.
LANDSCAPE USE Use in a large perennial or mixed border where it can provide lush foliage during summer and then in fall contribute bright pink flowers to the scene. Not a shy plant; the flowers can be seen from a distance.

Salvia 'Purple Majesty'

This lush, leafy hybrid has leaves similar to those of its *S. guaranitica* parent. The large trusses of rich purple flowers begin opening in midsummer and continue through fall.

TYPE, HABIT, AND SIZE A half-hardy perennial or shrub 4–6 feet (1.2–1.8 m) tall and wide.

HARDINESS Zone 9b

ORIGIN A hybrid between *S. guaranitica* and *S. gesneriiflora* 'Tequila'.

CULTIVATION Grow it in full sun in compost-amended soil and provide regular water. In hotter climates, it can be grown in partial shade. Plant growth can be rapid and soft, so watch for lanky branches that need cutting back during the growing season. In early to midspring, cut back hard to the woody stems.

LANDSCAPE USE Because of its leafiness and rich-colored flowers, 'Purple Majesty' and related hybrids of similar parentage blend well with other large, late-season perennials.

RELATED PLANTS

'Betsy's Purple' The most compact purple-flowered hybrid, growing to 3–5 feet (0.9–1.5 m) tall and wide. Good for container culture.

'Jean's Purple Passion' A huge plant at 9 feet (2.7 m) tall and nearly as wide.

Salvia purpurea

Purple sage

It is too bad this is so tender, so large, and winter flowering, although for gardeners in a mild climate who have the room, it is a glorious salvia to grow. It has a broad range, so there is, no doubt, much variability depending on the origin. The foliage is crisp and clean on slender woody stems. The flowers, which are a unique shade of warm orchid pink, begin to open in fall and continue through winter.

TYPE, HABIT, AND SIZE A tender shrub 8–12 feet (2.4–3.6 m) tall and 5–7 feet (1.5–2.1 m) wide.

HARDINESS Zone 10a

ORIGIN Central America

CULTIVATION Grow in filtered light or with afternoon shade in good humus-amended soil. Needs adequate water in the growing season to support the sizeable plant.

LANDSCAPE USE Best grown among medium to large shrubs that can lend support. Cut back in the spring to a woody framework.

Salvia radula

Multitudes of strongly vertical stems carry the hooded bright white flowers in summer and fall. The crinkled leaves are hairy and resinous with a pleasant scent. A showy perennial, this salvia provides strong form and flowers for the dry garden.

TYPE, HABIT, AND SIZE A tender upright-growing perennial 4 feet (1.2 m) tall and wide.

HARDINESS Zone 9b

ORIGIN South Africa

CULTIVATION Prefers well-drained, lean soil in full sun. It is drought tolerant, requiring little water.

LANDSCAPE USE *Salvia radula* provides strong structural contrast with other xeric plantings. The showy white flowers combined with the green foliage also contribute greatly.

Salvia 'Raspberry Royale'

A selection that is not only very showy when covered in rich raspberry-red flowers for much of the season, but one that has proven itself to be a durable grower, tolerant of heat, cold, and humidity.

TYPE, HABIT, AND SIZE A semievergreen subshrub making a rounded plant 2–3 feet (60–90 cm) tall and wide.
HARDINESS Zone 6
ORIGIN A selection in the *Salvia greggii/microphylla* complex.
CULTIVATION Full sun, well-drained soil, and little to moderate summer water.
LANDSCAPE USE A showy salvia that holds its own in large rock gardens, perennial borders, xeric gardens, and of course, containers.

Salvia 'Raspberry Truffle'▾

This salvia flower impresses with its very large spikes of deep raspberry-red flowers with dark purple calyces. The plant is large and leafy, blooming in midfall.

TYPE, HABIT, AND SIZE A half-hardy perennial 5–8 feet (1.5–1.8 m) tall and 5–7 feet (1.5–2.1 m) wide.
HARDINESS Zone 9a
ORIGIN A horticultural hybrid of *S. gesneriiflora* and *S. mexicana*.
CULTIVATION Grow in partial shade in hot climates, in good soil enriched with compost, and provide moderate water.
LANDSCAPE USE Effective in a perennial or mixed shrub border. Good for containers, although it blooms late in the year.

Salvia recognita▸

From a low woody base of foliage, the stiff flowering stems of this attractive plant carry a dozen or more whorls of pink flowers. Though only a few flowers open at one time, the resinous, hairy calyces catch the light, adding a translucent, ephemeral look. The dissected basal leaves are grayish green.

TYPE, HABIT, AND SIZE A hardy perennial with a woody basal leaf clump 12 inches (30 cm) tall and 18 inches (45 cm) wide and with flowering stems 24–30 inches (60–75 cm) tall.
HARDINESS Zone 6
ORIGIN Turkey
CULTIVATION Grows best in arid climates. Prefers very well drained, lean soil and occasional water in summer.
LANDSCAPE USE A perennial for the xeric landscape.

Salvia regla
Mountain sage

This is one impressive and interesting salvia. How many shrubs come into bloom around Halloween with masses of orange flowers? Mountain sage grows into a woody shrub with smallish leaves that are slightly wrinkled and heavily veined. The brightly colored orange flowers are held in matching calyces that emphasize the orange effect.

TYPE, HABIT, AND SIZE A half-hardy deciduous shrub 5–7 feet (1.5–2.1 m) tall and 4–7 feet (1.2–2.1 m) wide.

HARDINESS Zone 8a

ORIGIN Texas, Mexico.

CULTIVATION Grow it in full sun or partial shade. Once established it only requires occasional deep watering. It has different pruning requirements than most other salvias. To prune mountain sage, remove any dead stems when the plant has leafed out and then prune only to shape, leaving most of the existing structure.

LANDSCAPE USE Place the mountain sage in a quiet spot in the garden where the bright display of orange flowers in the fall seems unexpected and has no competition. Shrubs that bloom earlier in the year are good companions.

Salvia reptans ◄

This little wildflower salvia from Texas grows on you. The foliage is narrow and wispy—hardly there at all—but the small flowers are such an intense cobalt blue you cannot help but be taken in by them. There are essentially two forms of this species. One has very lax, nearly prostrate stems, while newer introductions have stems that are more vertical. Both versions run underground.

TYPE, HABIT, AND SIZE A hardy perennial 2 feet (0.6 m) tall and 4 feet (1.2 m) wide.
HARDINESS Zone 5
ORIGIN Texas
CULTIVATION Grow it in full sun in decent soil that drains well.
LANDSCAPE USE Fitting for a meadow, wildflower garden, or perennial border.

Salvia ringens ◄

In optimal growing conditions, this salvia makes stately stands of tall waving stems carrying violet-blue flowers. The flowering stems arise from a basal clump of hairy, gray-green divided leaves. Blooms appear in early summer.

TYPE, HABIT, AND SIZE A hardy perennial with a woody basal leaf clump 12 inches (30 cm) tall and 18 inches (45 cm) wide and with flowering stems to 4 feet (1.2 m) tall.
HARDINESS Zone 6
ORIGIN Balkans
CULTIVATION If planted in well-drained soil, *S. ringens* can tolerate regular watering in the growing season. Grows best in full sun.
LANDSCAPE USE Mixes well with other perennials as long as it is not crowded.

Salvia 'Robin Middleton'▲

The flowers are a lovely combination of very soft pink and white. The foliage is a rich green, and the plant is low and compact.

TYPE, HABIT, AND SIZE A small shrubby salvia to 24 inches (60 cm) tall and 30 inches (75 cm) wide.

HARDINESS Zone 7b

ORIGIN One of the many selections of the *Salvia greggii/microphylla* complex.

CULTIVATION Grow in partial shade to highlight the delicate coloring of the flowers . As with other plants in the group, provide well-drained soil and regular, but moderate water during the growing season. Trim back lightly during the growing season.

LANDSCAPE USE Ideal plant for a container where the flowers can be viewed up close, or planted at the feet of taller shrubs that will provide some shade.

Salvia rubescens ◄

This handsome, long-blooming perennial has long vertical wands of orange-red flowers set in nearly black calyces. The large leaves are heavily textured with a slight silver cast.

TYPE, HABIT, AND SIZE A tender perennial 5–6 feet (1.5–1.8 m) tall and 4 feet (1.2 m) wide.
HARDINESS Zone 10a
ORIGIN Venezuela, Colombia.
CULTIVATION Prefers well-drained soil with compost added and regular water throughout the growing season. Remove older spent flowers.
LANDSCAPE USE In most climates, this species will begin to flower in late summer and continue through fall, which makes it ideal to place in perennial or mixed borders where the tall flower stems will take up some slack after summer flowers have passed. Elegant and showy.

Salvia sagittata ▲

A good plant for foliage and an outstanding plant for blue flowers. The large, textured leaves are somewhat arrow-shaped with downy white hairs on the underside. The flowers are an intense Prussian blue on stems that rise well above the foliage.

TYPE, HABIT, AND SIZE A tender perennial with foliage 2 feet (0.6 m) tall and 4 feet (1.2 m) wide and flowering stems to 3 feet (0.9 m) tall.
HARDINESS Zone 10a
ORIGIN South America
CULTIVATION Grow it in full sun; give partial shade in hot climates. Needs good, well-drained soil with regular water in the growing season.
LANDSCAPE USE Container culture works well where the lush spreading plant can billow out over the edges. The flowers of this species are considered by some to be among the best blues in the salvia world.

Salvia 'Sally Greenwood'

This vigorous hybrid has small bright green leaves and masses of purple-blue flowers. Spreading underground, it can quickly make a solid cover 3 feet (0.9 m) across.

TYPE, HABIT, AND SIZE A half-hardy perennial 15 inches (38 cm) tall and 3–4 feet (90–120 cm) wide.

HARDINESS Zone 8b

ORIGIN A hybrid between two Mexican species, *S. coahuilensis* and *S. chamaedryoides*.

CULTIVATION Provide full sun to light shade in well-drained soil. This salvia is fairly drought tolerant, yet can tolerate frequent irrigation. Cut back hard in late winter, and trim lightly as needed to keep tidy in the growing season.

LANDSCAPE USE A wonderful salvia to use for softening the edges of paving and pathways or among large rocks.

Salvia 'Savannah Blue'. ▲

This hybrid brings the finely cut, fresh green foliage of
S. namaensis on a smaller plant with flowers that are more
prominent. The flowering stems sweep upward, carrying
the airy spikes of small, light blue flowers. 'Savannah Blue'
has a very tidy, attractive habit.

TYPE, HABIT, AND SIZE An evergreen shrub in mild
climates, more perennial in habit if winter temperatures fall
much below 25°F (-4°C). It grows 30 inches (75 cm) tall
and wide.

HARDINESS Zone 9a

ORIGIN A hybrid of South African species *S. namaensis* and
S. repens.

CULTIVATION Grow it in full sun. It is drought tolerant, but
not fussy about water. Trim back spent flowering stems
during the growing season.

LANDSCAPE USE This salvia lends a fresh green look to the
dry garden whether used singly or planted in a sweep. It
contrasts nicely with the silvery gray foliage of some of the
California native salvias or other Mediterranean plants.

Salvia sclarea ◄

Clary sage

Clary sage has been a popular salvia for many years in herb gardens and perennial borders. It makes a broad rough clump of basal leaves up to 2 feet (60 cm) across. In early summer, the very showy inflorescence opens well above the basal leaves. Although the flowers are quite small, the colored bracts, in gradations from white to pink, attract attention. This species is considered an invasive weed in the state of Washington, where preventing new infestations and eradicating existing infestations should be considered.

TYPE, HABIT, AND SIZE A hardy biennial 2 feet (60 cm) tall and 2–4 feet (60–120 cm) wide.
HARDINESS Zone 5
ORIGIN Mediterranean
CULTIVATION Grow it in full sun in well-drained soil. As a biennial, Clary sage usually dies after flowering and producing seed, but it can be a short-lived perennial. Can reseed prolifically and will survive with little water.
LANDSCAPE USE Clary sage is effective in herb gardens, perennial gardens, and xeric gardens. Place it where it can be viewed when backlit by the sun. The plant literally glows with the low light shining through the translucent bracts. This sage lends an old-fashioned, cottage flavor to the garden and some drama when in peak bloom.

Salvia semiatrata ▲

I have often wished this sage were a bit hardier so I could enjoy it in my garden. It makes a relatively small, many-branched, woody shrub. The leaves are barely an inch (2.5 cm) long and are pebbled on the surface and along the leaf margins. The inflorescences are short and abundantly produced with an interesting blend of colors. The tubular flower is violet colored washed with white, while the lower petal is solid violet, creating a two-toned effect. The prominent calyces, covered with little hairs, are a dusky rose. The plant flowers from summer into fall.

TYPE, HABIT, AND SIZE A tender shrub 4–5 feet (1.2–1.5 m) tall and 3–4 feet (0.9–1.2 m) wide.
HARDINESS Zone 9b
ORIGIN Mexico
CULTIVATION Grow it in full sun to partial shade, in good well-drained soil. Thin and prune as needed during the growing season.
LANDSCAPE USE This tidy shrub is suitable for a container or partially shaded shrub border. The flowers are many, yet subtle, so they are best positioned where they can be enjoyed close-up.

Salvia sinaloensis ◄

Sinaloa sage

A low, compact salvia striking for its contrast of reddish purple tinged leaves and spikes of intense deep blue flowers. Two prominent white pollinator guides brighten the overall effect of the flowers.

TYPE, HABIT, AND SIZE A half-hardy perennial 8 inches (20 cm) tall and 18 inches (45 cm) wide.
HARDINESS Zone 9b
ORIGIN Mexico
CULTIVATION In hot summer areas, *S. sinaloensis* grows best in partial shade. However, in too much shade the purple cast of the leaves will fade. The species prefers good humus-rich soil and regular irrigation.
LANDSCAPE USE It is easily adaptable to use in the front of perennial or shrub borders where, with its dark purple tinted foliage, it provides depth and contrast. It also does very well in container plantings. Being herbaceous, it dies to the ground in the winter and can be late to emerge in the spring.

Salvia somalensis ▲

Somalia sage

Somalia sage has a different look than most of the South African shrubby salvias. The fragrant, leathery leaves are much larger at nearly 4 inches (10 cm) long, and the lavender-blue flowers open on longer flowering stalks held above the foliage. The plant has a substantial, hardy look.

TYPE, HABIT, AND SIZE An evergreen shrub 3–5 feet (0.9–1.5 m) tall and wide.
HARDINESS Zone 8b
ORIGIN South Africa
CULTIVATION Grow it in full sun to partial shade. Accepts moderate amounts of water as long as the soil is well drained.
LANDSCAPE USE The large leaves and the overall midgreen appearance can bring some contrast to the often small, gray leaves of many drought-tolerant plants. Effective in mixed borders or as an accent plant in the xeric garden.

Salvia sonomensis
Creeping sage

Creeping sage is a fast-growing groundcover that makes a low dense mat of silvery gray leaves. The showy flowers are held in stacked whorls on 10-inch (25-cm) stems. The flower color can be in varying shades of blue. The strongly scented foliage also varies in color, from quite silvery to greener, depending on the origin of the plant.

TYPE, HABIT, AND SIZE An evergreen groundcover 8 inches (20 cm) tall and spreading 5 feet (1.5 m).

HARDINESS Zone 6a

ORIGIN California

CULTIVATION Good drainage and little to no summer water is required. Some winter dieback can occur if the soil is too wet and cold. The plant appreciates some relief from all-day sun.

LANDSCAPE USE Use as a low-growing groundcover on slopes and banks (see photo on page 29).

Salvia spathacea
Hummingbird sage

This California native has a habit that is unique from other native sages. Hummingbird sage spreads underground, colonizing an area with its rhizomatous stems. It forms a dense carpet of large, textured arrowhead-shaped leaves that are lightly sticky and have a distinctive sweet, pungent fragrance. In winter, the foliage is sparse, and as spring progresses the number and size of leaves increases and the flowering stalks rise. Large maroon-red flowers poke out of the dense calyces, which are also maroon tinted, as are the leaf bracts that subtend the calyx.

TYPE, HABIT, AND SIZE An evergreen perennial with a foliage clump 6 inches (15 cm) tall and spreading to 5 feet (1.5 m) across and with flowering stems 18–48 inches (45–120 cm) tall, depending on the cultivar.

HARDINESS Zone 8b

ORIGIN California

CULTIVATION Prefers partial shade, near the shade of large shrubs, or under oak trees. Needs little water, though some irrigation in summer freshens up the foliage. Remove old flower stalks as desired to keep plants tidy.

LANDSCAPE USE Hummingbird sage is useful for covering the ground between larger perennials (such as yarrow, see photo), shrubs, or grasses, or as an understory plant under oaks. It is very drought tolerant and thrives in half sun, appreciating some afternoon shade.

RELATED PLANTS

'Avis Keedy' Selected from a native population for its creamy yellow fading to near white flowers.

'Powerline Pink' Noted for its tall flowering stems to 3–5 feet (90–150 cm). As the plant's name suggests, the flowers of this horticultural selection are magenta-pink.

Salvia spathacea
'Cerro Alto'▸

Peachy, apricot-colored flowers on this vigorous selection of the hummingbird sage make it an unusual addition to the dry shade garden. It makes a low carpet of large fragrant leaves.

TYPE, HABIT, AND SIZE An evergreen groundcover 3–4 feet (90–120 cm) across with flowering stems 18 inches (45 cm) tall.

HARDINESS Zone 8b

ORIGIN California

CULTIVATION Grow in partial shade with occasional irrigation in the summer. Shear spent flowering stems whenever they become unattractive. Each gardener has his or her own tolerance for neatness.

LANDSCAPE USE An excellent plant for dry shade under oaks, or other large trees with open shade, or at the base of chaparral-type shrubs, such as ceanothus, manzanita, and toyon. This selection is best enjoyed along a path where the subtle color can be appreciated in closer view.

Salvia splendens ▲
Scarlet sage

Once upon a time, nearly 200 years ago, *Salvia splendens* was a wild and varied plant growing up to 9 feet (2.7 m) tall. Then the horticulturists began their work. They selected and hybridized, as they continue to do today, creating very compact, very floriferous varieties that come in colors of red, pink, salmon, white, and bicolor. These are popular bedding-out annuals that are tidy and that bloom nonstop from late spring through fall. Many seed strains are available and can be selected for color and size.

TYPE, HABIT, AND SIZE A tender perennial 18 inches (45 cm) tall and 12 inches (30 cm) wide.

HARDINESS Zone 10a

ORIGIN Brazil

CULTIVATION These bedding annuals are nearly indestructible. Grow it in full sun and good soil, and give a moderate amount of water. Deadhead (remove old flowers) as needed to encourage continued flowering.

LANDSCAPE USE With their formal appearance, the bedding varieties look best in mass plantings with other annuals. They are perfect for growing in pots where a long season of bloom is desired.

RELATED PLANTS

'Peach' Grows 3–4 feet (0.9–1.2 m) tall and bears peachy flowers in summer and fall.

'Sao Borja' Grows fast and large, to 6 feet (1.8 m) tall. The flowers and calyces are a dusky burgundy-purple.

Salvia splendens 'Van Houttei' ▲
Van Houtte's sage

This old selection of *S. splendens* has survived through the years. It has a loose habit, growing quite freely through summer. In late summer, the inflorescences begin to show their deep burgundy bracts. Gradually the carmine flowers appear, combining to make a colorful, long-lasting display until frost. Hummingbirds love the richly colored flowers.

TYPE, HABIT, AND SIZE A tender perennial forming a loose mound 3–4 feet (0.9–1.2 m) tall and wide.

HARDINESS Zone 10a

ORIGIN Brazil

CULTIVATION Give plenty of water during the growing season. Needs some shade from the afternoon heat. 'Van Houttei' can sprawl and become entwined with neighboring plants. If a more compact plant is desired, tip prune during the summer.

LANDSCAPE USE Plant as a large annual in any climate. It is lovely in grouped container plantings where its long, loose branches can relax and intertwine with companions.

Salvia subrotunda

Frequently recommended as a good salvia for humming-birds, this fast-growing plant is continually in bloom from late spring through fall. The small, tubular, soft orange flowers are scattered throughout this well-branched salvia, giving it a delicate and airy appearance. Grow this sage as an annual in any climate.

TYPE, HABIT, AND SIZE A tender salvia 3–5 feet (0.9–1.5 m) tall and wide.
HARDINESS Zone 10a
ORIGIN Brazil
CULTIVATION Grow it in full sun to partial shade in hot climates. Requires a well-drained soil that is amended with compost.
LANDSCAPE USE This species is well suited for container culture with its long bloom season.

Salvia ×sylvestris 'Caradonna'

One of the best hybrids of *S. ×sylvestris*, with a strong vertical habit of glowing purple-black stems and violet-purple flowers. Very striking in the landscape when in bloom mid to late spring.

TYPE, HABIT, AND SIZE A hardy herbaceous perennial 18 inches (45 cm) tall and nearly as wide.

HARDINESS Zone 4

ORIGIN A hybrid between Eurasian species.

CULTIVATION Grow it in full sun to light shade in well-drained soil. Survives with little water, but looks best and will rebloom with moderate irrigation. Remove spent flowers to encourage a second flowering.

LANDSCAPE USE A prominent salvia for use in the perennial border where the verticality of the stiff stems and the richly colored flowers make for some strong combinations with yellow yarrow and daylilies or interspersed with roses.

Salvia ×sylvestris 'Mainacht'

SYNONYM 'May Night'

Of the hardy salvias, this cultivar is without question the most popular. It is a showy, undemanding perennial that blooms for many weeks beginning in late spring and often continuing through summer. The flowers are a dark violet-blue against darker bracts. The tidy, colorful plants are excellent for attracting bees and butterflies.

TYPE, HABIT, AND SIZE A hardy perennial 12–36 inches (30–90 cm) tall and 12–18 inches (30–45 cm) wide.
HARDINESS Zone 5
ORIGIN A horticultural hybrid from Germany.
CULTIVATION 'Mainacht' and related cultivars grow best in full sun and well-drained soil amended with compost. Provide moderate summer water for these drought-tolerant salvias. During the growing season, remove old flower stems to encourage more flowers.
LANDSCAPE USE Perennial borders, cottage gardens, with roses, container plantings.
RELATED PLANTS
'Blue Hill' Synonym 'Blauhügel'. Midblue flowers.
'East Friesland' Synonym 'Ostfriesland'. Violet flowers, lighter than 'Mainacht'. May flop a bit later in the season.
'Plumosa' Unique for its plumelike inflorescence and mauve, rosy pink flowers on stems 15 inches (38 cm) tall.
'Rose Queen' Rosy pink flower spikes to 18 inches (45 cm) tall.
'Tänzerin' Violet-blue flowers against darker bracts. A good cultivar.
'Viola Klose' Intense dark blue flowers on stems 15–18 inches (38–45 cm) tall.

Salvia ×*sylvestris* '**Merleau Blue**'

A tight-growing compact plant with deeply colored, purplish blue flowers in short spikes.

TYPE, HABIT, AND SIZE A hardy herbaceous perennial, making a small clump of deep green leaves 10 inches (25 cm) across, with flower spikes to 10 inches (25 cm) tall.
HARDINESS Zone 4
ORIGIN A hybrid between Eurasian species.
CULTIVATION Grow it in full sun to light shade in well-drained soil. Survives with little water, but looks best and will rebloom with moderate irrigation.
LANDSCAPE USE Plant in drifts of three plants or more and repeat in the front of a perennial, mixed shrub or rose border. It would be striking in front of yellow yarrow.

Salvia ×*sylvestris* 'Schneehügel' ◂

SYNONYM 'Snow Hill'

Clean, crisp white flowers smother the upright stems in late spring. The neat clump of foliage is light green. A superb white-flowering perennial.

TYPE, HABIT, AND SIZE A hardy herbaceous perennial 16 inches (40 cm) tall and 18 inches (45 cm) wide.
HARDINESS Zone 4
ORIGIN A hybrid between Eurasian species.
CULTIVATION Grow it in full sun to light shade in well-drained soil. All the cultivars of *S.* ×*sylvestris* survive with little water, but look best and rebloom with moderate irrigation. Remove spent flowers to encourage reblooming.
LANDSCAPE USE Perfect for the front of the perennial border or brightening an area against green shrubs.

Salvia 'Tangerine Ballet' ▴

Bright salmon-orange flowers with a touch of yellow smother this plant for periods from spring to fall. This cultivar is a unique color selection in the *S. greggii/ microphylla* complex and very showy.

TYPE, HABIT, AND SIZE A semievergreen, upright-growing woody subshrub 3–4 feet (90–120 cm) tall and not quite as wide.
HARDINESS Zone 7b
ORIGIN One of the many selections of the *S. greggii/ microphylla* complex.
CULTIVATION Needs full sun to light shade, good drainage, and occasional deep watering in the summer. Trim periodically in the growing season, and prune hard (cut back halfway) in early spring.
LANDSCAPE USE Planted in groups of three or more makes for a brilliant display, whether surrounded by the silvery grays of lavender or the purples of berberis.

Salvia taraxacifolia

Dandelion sage

As the common name suggests, this salvia resembles the common dandelion, specifically in its leaves, which are narrow, incised, and grow in a tight basal cluster. The flowering stems carry few-flowered whorls with flowers that are a beautiful combination of creamy yellow and soft pink. These are not large or showy, but they are lovely.

TYPE, HABIT, AND SIZE A half-hardy perennial with a foliage clump 2 inches (5 cm) tall and 6 inches (15 cm) across and with flowering stems 10–16 inches (25–40 cm) tall.
HARDINESS Zone 8a
ORIGIN Morocco
CULTIVATION Prefers well-drained soil with compost added and regular water throughout the growing season. Remove older spent flowers.
LANDSCAPE USE The small stature of the dandelion sage makes it suitable for establishment along a gravel path or in a small rock garden.

Salvia thymoides
Thyme-leaved sage

The species name is fitting, as the diminutive, soft gray-green leaves are no bigger than those of common thyme. The flowers are a soft lavender-blue with two splashes of white on the broad lower lip. While the plant never has quantities of flowers open at once, there are always a few blooms sprinkled around the plant.

TYPE, HABIT, AND SIZE A half-hardy shrublet 8 inches (20 cm) tall and 12 inches (30 cm) wide.
HARDINESS Zone 9a
ORIGIN Mexico
CULTIVATION Grow it in full sun to light shade in well-drained soil.
LANDSCAPE USE Very appropriate for a small rock garden or in containers.

Salvia tomentosa

Although not commonly grown, this salvia makes a very natural looking, loose but tidy colony of stems clothed in 3-inch (7.5-cm) long green leaves. Each stem is topped with a loose spike of large, pale blue flowers. When I saw this salvia growing at Denver Botanic Gardens, it was planted in the shade around the base of a large cedar. In a sunny position, the flowers might have looked pale, but they certainly lit up this shady spot in early summer.

TYPE, HABIT, AND SIZE A hardy perennial 18 inches (45 cm) tall and 24 inches (60 cm) wide.
HARDINESS Zone 6
ORIGIN Balkans
CULTIVATION Grow it in full sun to shade in soil with good drainage and amended with compost. Needs moderate watering.
LANDSCAPE USE Particularly effective in a woodland garden or partially shaded perennial border.

Salvia transsylvanica

A strong-growing perennial with coarse, deep green basal leaves. In early summer, the much-branched inflorescence carries closely arranged deep purple-blue flowers. This is a showy salvia in bloom.

TYPE, HABIT, AND SIZE A hardy perennial 3–4 feet (90–120 cm) tall and 2–3 feet (60–90 cm) wide.
HARDINESS Zone 5
ORIGIN Eastern Europe
CULTIVATION This tough plant is tolerant of many conditions from xeric to moderate irrigation. Grow it in full sun to partial shade.
LANDSCAPE USE Perennial borders with tall yarrows and daylilies.

Salvia uliginosa
Bog sage

"Willowy, waving wands" describe the essence of this species. Forming a thicket of tall slender stems and narrow leaves, bog sage bears racemes of clear, sky blue flowers atop slender stems in summer and fall. The flowers are beautiful, but the plant is not tidy. Bog sage spreads vigorously and within a few years easily reaches full mature size. It is a good plant for bees.

TYPE, HABIT, AND SIZE A hardy perennial with spreading growth 6 feet (1.8 m) tall and wide.
HARDINESS Zone 6a
ORIGIN South America
CULTIVATION Grows best in partial shade. Requires regular water, but does not need boggy conditions as its common name suggests. Cut the plant to the ground in spring.
LANDSCAPE USE The height and spreading habit of bog sage determine its placement in the garden. Plant with strong-growing perennials such as *Rudbeckia* 'Autumn Sun', helianthus, tall grasses, and other large salvias.

Salvia verticillata 'Purple Rain'

A consistently popular hardy salvia grown primarily for its combined look of foliage and flowers. This leafy plant has large leaves with short hairs giving them a soft fuzzy look. The often-arching inflorescences are set with many close whorls of rosy mauve bracts highlighted with small mauve-pink flowers. The two floral shades do not make a dramatic combination, but rather one that lends a quiet, colorful appearance.

TYPE, HABIT, AND SIZE A hardy perennial 30 inches (75 cm) tall and wide.
HARDINESS Zone 5
ORIGIN Central Europe
CULTIVATION Grows best in full sun in good friable soil with moderate water during the growing season. Remove spent flowering stems to encourage more flowers.
LANDSCAPE USE Enhances mixed perennial plantings. Combines well with rudbeckias, helianthus, grasses, and asters.

Salvia vitifolia▸
Grape leaf sage

Large, downy midgreen leaves with a pronounced shape of grape leaves are reason alone to grow this salvia as a foliage plant. However, the flowers are also a huge draw; they are very large and a very pure, clear, deep blue. An impressive plant in all aspects.

TYPE, HABIT, AND SIZE A half-hardy perennial 3–5 feet (0.9–1.5 m) tall and wide.
HARDINESS Zone 9a
ORIGIN Oaxaca (state) in Mexico.
CULTIVATION Such a lush plant requires shade, plenty of water, and rich, yet well-drained soil.
LANDSCAPE USE An excellent plant for a large container, where it will grow up and spill over with luxuriant foliage.

Salvia wagneriana▸
Wagner sage

This is a handsome salvia. The leaves are large, held prominently by strong petioles, and clothe the plant from top to bottom. In late autumn, the flowers begin to form. There are at least two forms of this species, one has rose-pink bracts (see photo on page 15), and the other white bracts (pictured). These prominent bracts sheath the young inflorescence, which gradually unfolds to reveal coral-pink flowers with a white lower lip. The color combination is exquisite.

TYPE, HABIT, AND SIZE A tender shrub 8–12 feet (2.4–3.6 m) tall and 6–8 feet (1.8–2.4 m) wide.
HARDINESS Zone 10a
ORIGIN Central America
CULTIVATION Grow in light shade in the usual, good compost-enhanced soil, and supply regular irrigation. This beautiful salvia needs a near frost-free climate; in colder climates, grow it in a greenhouse.
LANDSCAPE USE Makes a specimen plant in a large garden where it can be given space.

Salvia viridis▴

While the tiny pink flowers are barely discernible, the white, pink, or purple modified leaf bracts are very noticeable and are the reason for growing this species. Popular as a cut flower, *S. viridis* makes a lovely filler in fresh bouquets as well as in in dried arrangements.

TYPE, HABIT, AND SIZE An annual 24 inches (60 cm) tall and 12 inches (30 cm) wide.
HARDINESS All zones as an annual.
ORIGIN Mediterranean
CULTIVATION Grow it in full sun in good well-drained soil. It is easy to start plants from seed, sown either in place or in pots in midspring.
LANDSCAPE USE Cut flower garden, containers, herb garden, and mixed borders, especially cottagey perennial borders.

Salvia 'Waverly'

Elegant is the word I use to describe this hybrid. The word suggests clean, pleasing lines, grace, and subtlety—qualities exemplified by the unified foliage and flowers of 'Waverly'. The foliage is slightly textured and deep green. The long, arching branches terminate with wands of white, pink-flushed flowers contrasting with stonewashed burgundy bracts. Clean, fresh, and attractive all season, this salvia begins blooming in summer and continues well into fall or until the first hard freeze.

TYPE, HABIT, AND SIZE A tender perennial 4–5 feet (1.2–1.5 m) tall and 4–6 feet (1.2–1.8 m) wide.
HARDINESS Zone 9a
ORIGIN A garden hybrid.
CULTIVATION Prefers some afternoon shade in hot summer climates and does best with regular water.
LANDSCAPE USE Being one of the fast-growing, tender salvias, 'Waverly' can be used as a long-blooming annual in all zones or as a perennial plant in mild-climate gardens. It is easy to site in mixed borders or to use as a specimen container plant. Although this hybrid may not be the showiest salvia, its soft colors are gorgeous close-up or shown off to advantage when planted in front of bolder foliage or dense green shrubs.

Salvia 'Wendy's Wish'

'Wendy's Wish' makes an open, yet tidy plant, with 2-inch (5-cm) long green leaves overlaying maroon veining. The stems of the plant are also maroon and, from late spring through fall, produce large, loose clusters of purplish red flowers held, again loosely, by papery, dusty pink bracts. This is a wonderful plant for hummingbirds and carpenter bees who find it in the early morning.

TYPE, HABIT, AND SIZE A tender perennial 3–4 feet (0.9–1.2 m) tall and wide.
HARDINESS Zone 9a
ORIGIN A seedling from Australia.
CULTIVATION Grow it in full sun, except in hot climates where it will need some shade. Give it well-drained soil and moderate water. Remove old flowers to encourage more flowering, and trim back stray lanky branches.
LANDSCAPE USE An excellent container plant and easily placed in a mixed border. Because the flowers are on the dark side, they tend to recede in the landscape.

GROWING AND PROPAGATING

For sustained color in a late summer border, pair the indigo blue flowers of *Salvia guaranitica* with the bold foliage of canna.

T

Through the years, I have learned which salvias I can grow that give me great pleasure with little investment—those that endure the winters and long, hot, dry summers without a lot of fuss. I also know which salvias I do not mind fussing over, whether that means giving them extra water in summer and some shade. A third group includes the salvias I am willing to gamble on overwintering successfully, because enjoying the flowers in late summer and fall is well worth the cost and the minimal effort invested. You too will quickly discover which salvias thrive in your landscape and which require additional effort.

There are no hard-and-fast rules about salvia cultivation. These plants have been brought into our landscape from many different regions of the world—from the 8000-foot (2400-m) elevations of South American cloud forests to the hot, low-rainfall mountains of southern California, from the cold, dry steppes of Turkey and the Caucasus to the rocky slopes of the Himalayas, from European meadows to Asian forests. Despite all this remarkable diversity of habitats, salvias are, as a rule, easily grown plants.

Salvia candelabrum, a Mediterranean species, appreciates the well-drained soil of raised beds in the Sacramento Historic City Cemetary.

Soils and Irrigation

Salvias are generally highly adaptable, easy plants. When we plant them in our gardens, we are planting them not to just survive, but to look colorful and grow vigorously. It all begins with healthy soil conditions.

Well drained is perhaps the most frequently used phrase in this book. Nearly all salvias grow best in well-drained soils that do not hold water too long. This does not mean a soil has to be sandy or gravelly. It means that water needs to percolate through the soil at a reasonable rate. Some soils have such high clay content, or have a layer of hardpan underlying the top soil layer, or have been so compacted by heavy equipment during construction that, if a hole is dug and filled with water, most of the water will be there a few hours later. That is not a good situation for any salvia. Salvias do not like wet feet for long either in the growing season or in winter.

Good drainage is especially necessary for the species that originate from Mediterranean climates. These dryland plants are adapted to surviving long periods with little or no precipitation and can be susceptible to fungal issues when the soil becomes warm and moist in summer. This problem commonly occurs when gardeners grow English lavender (*Lavandula angustifolia*), a Mediterranean species despite the common name that would seem to indicate otherwise. In my experience, most people lose their lavenders in

In this nonirrigated Denver parking strip, *Salvia recognita* and *S. cyanescens* thrive along with gaillardia, iris, and yarrow.

the hottest part of the summer not from lack of water, but from thinking that the plants need more water and then oversaturating the soil.

Growing Mediterranean salvias in soil with less-than-optimal drainage is not impossible, however. Raising the soil level 3–6 inches (7.5–15.0 cm) makes a difference in a plant's health and winter survival rate. Low mounds or raised beds can help by generating positive drainage around a plant's crown and by aerating the soil. Also pay attention to the watering so that soils do not become saturated, especially during hot spells. It is better to allow plants to be stressed by lack of water than to give them a long soak under the wrong circumstances. Water regularly and lightly during the heat of summer. An occasional deep soaking may be good for many salvias, but not the Mediterranean species.

Some salvias are fussier than others about drainage, in which case special beds (think rock garden) or even containers can be prepared for them. The salvias that Panayoti Kelaidis recommends for rock gardens (see sidebar on page 31), along with a few others such as *Salvia pachyphylla* and *S. dorrii*, benefit from increased drainage. Small sharp gravel blended into the soil and used as a topping will increase chances for healthy growth.

There are no fixed rules on the frequency of watering Mediterranean salvias or the way in which water is applied. It all depends on soil type, climate, the particular plant, and the gardener. Allow the soil to dry out between waterings. It is always best for xeric plants to err on the side of too dry.

The hardy perennial salvias, often from Europe and Asia, also like soil that drains well. However, they perform best if the soil is richer than the soil needed by Mediterranean-type salvias. For these hardy Eurasian salvias, amending the soil with compost, in whatever form, is helpful. This should be done at the initial planting, followed by mulching around the plants with compost in the fall or early spring in subsequent years. Heavy, wet soil, particularly in winter, shortens the life of even the toughest salvia.

Salvias for Hot, Humid Climates

RICHARD DUFRESNE, ONE of the foremost salvia experts in the United States, gardens in North Carolina and recommends the following salvias for climates where summers are warm and humidity is high.

Salvia 'Anthony Parker'
Salvia 'Big Swing'
Salvia blepharophylla 'Painted Lady'
Salvia greggii 'Alba'
Salvia greggii 'Furman's Red'
Salvia guaranitica cultivars
Salvia 'Hot Lips'
Salvia 'Indigo Spires'
Salvia leucantha
Salvia madrensis
Salvia mexicana
Salvia microphylla 'San Carlos Festival'
Salvia 'Phyllis' Fancy'
Salvia 'Raspberry Royale'
Salvia reptans

Salvia pachyphylla and *S. fruticosa* are well matched for a container where the garden soil may be heavy for these dryland salvias.

Adding compost and mulching yearly will help increase life in the soil and over time will change the soil texture and aid in improving the drainage.

The hardy salvias appreciate moderate amounts of water in the growing season. *Salvia ×sylvestris* hybrids can endure dry conditions, but they look healthier, brighter, and bloom longer when not stressed for water.

Most of the tropical salvias benefit from soil that is improved by the addition of some compost or humus. Mulch is always beneficial, whether a layer of leaves from deciduous trees, composted manure, or bark-based compost. Many of these salvias are leafy plants and they transpire a fair amount of water on a hot, dry summer day. Good, friable soil enables the roots to spread down and out, making it easier for the plant to sustain itself.

Some of the tropical salvias are quite lush and grow quickly. These will need additional water throughout the growing season. *Salvia elegans*, for example, can wilt drastically, only to perk up when water is added. *Salvia madrensis* has large leaves and substantial stems. It is easy to visualize the water being pumped up through those stems to keep the plant growing. It clearly is not a plant that likes to be deprived of water.

The amount of water that tropical salvias require will very much depend on the climate. A salvia growing in a hot, humid or marine climate will need less water than one being grown in a hot arid or semiarid region.

Exposure: Sun and Shade

Whether to plant a salvia in full sun or shade or somewhere in between is dependent on the local climate. The description of a plant purchased from an area where summers are cool and often overcast may suggest the plant thrives in full sun. Bring that plant to hot arid conditions and it will struggle without a bit of shade.

Knowing the origin of the plant can be a helpful guide for understanding its placement in the garden. Tropical, cloud forest plants will require some shade. Plants native to California and the Mediterranean usually require a good amount of sun. Most can accept some leeway in either direction.

Another factor is neighboring plants. Often just that bit of shade and protection from a nearby plant makes a difference in the health and appearance of a salvia. Many of the little shrubby salvias that are said to grow in full sun, such as *Salvia lycioides*, appreciate being shaded at some point during the day. While their native habitat might be considered sunny as opposed to forested, it usually includes large shrubs or small trees to modify the sun's intensity, or changes in terrain that create little microclimates.

The large leaves of *Salvia gravida* indicate this plant might need some extra irrigation.

California Native Salvias

LILI SINGER, HORTICULTURIST with the Theodore Payne Foundation for Wildflowers and Native Plants in Sun Valley, California, recommends the following California native plants.

Salvia apiana
Salvia 'Bee's Bliss'
Salvia brandegeei 'Pacific Blue'
Salvia columbariae
Salvia 'Desperado'
Salvia mellifera 'Terra Seca'
Salvia pachyphylla
Salvia spathacea

Salvia 'Raspberry Royale' was selected by salvia expert Richard Dufresne for its ability to endure in a hot, humid climate.

Container Culture

Growing salvias in containers is a wonderful way to bring them up close, to enjoy their colorful flowers, their interesting foliage, and the wildlife they attract. There are small salvias that can be planted with other plants as textural or flower complements, and there are large, bold, long-blooming salvias to be planted in containers on their own.

The larger salvias are best planted in large pots filled with a water-retentive soil mix. Many commercial soil mixes are so light and fast draining that a large plant may need watering multiple times during the day once it fills the pot with roots. Mixing some heavier garden soil with a commercial mix helps to slow the root development, thus requiring less frequent watering.

Having access to adequate nutrients is necessary for the healthy growth of any container-grown plant, and salvias are no exception. In container culture there is a fine line between encouraging too much growth and having sufficient nutrients for slow, steady growth. A balanced slow-release organic fertilizer with additional feedings of fish emulsion or compost teas will ensure the plants have what they need. Be sure to water newly planted containers thoroughly, and be sure the pot has drainage holes before you fill it.

Hardiness

The cold hardiness zones for salvias described in this book range from Zone 4 to Zone 10. Most of the plants are hardy to Zone 9 or 10, meaning they can survive a winter temperature no lower than 20°F (-7°C). One species is hardy to Zone 4 (-30°F/-34°C); the rest fall in between. However, there is no precise way to determine the hardiness zones for a particular salvia, as factors other than temperature determine whether a plant will survive.

The hardiness zones cited in the plant descriptions are on the conservative side. Many plants will actually grow in a colder zone, but there are so many variables, such as the moisture content and type of soil, how long the cold period lasts, whether a snow cover is present, whether a mulch has been applied, and how exposed the plant may be in the garden.

Here are a few things to consider when planting salvias to assist them in surviving the winter. Start by selecting a location with good drainage, not a low spot where water collects. If possible, place the salvia against the south wall of a house or fence. Choose a site near large rocks where plant roots may overwinter next to or underneath the rocks. Mulch the area with an airy material such as pine boughs. As a final precaution, consider covering plants with a protective cloth in winter.

A small tree-sized chilopsis provides the right amount of protection from hot midday sun for native groundcovering *Salvia spathacea* to prosper.

It can be tremendously disappointing to grow a plant through the year and have it reach the point of being full of buds and flowers just beginning to open—your anticipation is high—and then, oh no, an early freeze. What makes the situation more frustrating is that after only one or two nights of cold, another month or more of frost-free nights follows.

For gardeners in temperamental climates who want to enjoy some of the fall-blooming salvias, it is a good idea to have some protective cloth or row cover fabric on hand. It is relatively easy to drape this lightweight material over and cover a plant using some clothespins. Depending on the thickness of the fabric, it can provide from 2 to 6 degrees of frost protection. This simple task can extend the salvia season for weeks and even months in some cases, and is well worth the cost in time and money.

Pruning

The one general rule about pruning salvias, particularly the species from Mexico, Central and South America, is to wait until winter is over before cutting back any of the stems. The plants may look terrible, but be patient. If you are a landscaper, explain to your clients that if the plants are cut back earlier, they lose the winter protection of old stems and dried leaves. More importantly, new cuts expose the plants to fungus diseases that can kill the plant. It is best to wait until early spring or until new growth is visible before attempting a major pruning.

During the growing season, in the heat of summer after plants have been flowering for weeks, flower production may drop off, particularly during hot spells. This can be a time for pruning back long flower stems. Plants like *Salvia* 'Wendy's Wish' and *S.* 'John Whittlesey' can produce long inflorescences, which need to be trimmed to keep the plant tidy and to encourage new growth. Periodically cutting back these spent stems encourages more flowers and a longer flowering period.

Pests and Diseases

One of the positive things about growing salvias is that they are relatively free from pests and diseases. The key to keeping plants that way is to keep them healthy. In all my years of growing salvias commercially and in my garden, I have never had any issue with any pest or disease.

Some plants, such as *Salvia splendens* 'Van Houttei' or *S.* 'Waverly', are susceptible to white fly. When plants are lanky, have soft growth, and are located in a site with limited air circulation, they are particularly prone to attracting this pest. If you catch white fly populations early, you can reduce the damage they cause. Remove infected foliage, and

A seedling of *Salvia greggii* growing with fuchsia in Sandi Martin's garden.

Right plant, right place. Native to Mexico and Central America, *Salvia cinnabarina* thrives under a shade tree at Cabrillo College, Aptos, California.

A rambunctious combination of a large *Salvia greggii*, nepeta, and the chartreuse sweet potato vine in front of the Plant Barn in Chico, California.

Salvia 'John Whittlesey' displaying its floriferous, unruly nature, and, as is usually the case, a hummingbird is in the vicinity.

treat the rest of the plant with organic soap and/or oil. Hanging yellow sticky traps helps control white fly populations when used before infestations become too large.

Red spider mites can also attack some species of salvias. These pests are difficult to control and a nuisance, but other than discoloring a plant's leaves, they rarely cause severe damage. Hosing the underside of the leaf is helpful, but not always possible. Predatory mites are very helpful in controlling populations of red spider mites.

Powdery mildew can occur on some salvias. This fungus usually develops from poor watering and growing conditions. By planting your salvias in the right light conditions and watering appropriately, powdery mildew should not be an issue.

Propagation

One reason salvias are and have been so popular is that they are easy plants to share, whether between gardening friends or big wholesale nurseries. They are, for the most part, easy to propagate, be it from seed, cuttings, or division.

Salvias are usually easy from seed, which is why there is an ever-increasing number of hybrids. Standard methods of sowing seeds apply whether to the annual salvias from seed catalogs or seed-collected plants at home.

Taking softwood cuttings is the usual practice for propagating salvias. Softwood cuttings are taken from young, but firm tip growth—usually before flowering, but they can be taken all through the growing season. Timing for taking cuttings is dependent on the growth habits of individual species. Spring-flowering salvias such as *Salvia ×sylvestris* hybrids only produce cutting material very early in the season, well before flowers begin to form in the young shoots.

For the salvias that spread by colonizing through their rhizomatous roots, or those with a leafy clump that slowly increases in size, the best choice for propagation is by division. This is done usually in the spring or the fall—not while the plant is flowering and at the height of its growing season.

One way to overwinter tender perennial salvias is to take softwood cuttings of favorite plants and root them indoors. The best time to take softwood cuttings is in late summer or early fall, before the stems have hardened. Often in the fall, it is not easy to find optimum cutting material as many of the stems tips have flowered, so it may be necessary to look down into the plant to find strong, nonflowering tip growth.

Using a sharp, sterilized knife, cut several nonflowering stems with 3 or 4 sets of leaves. Take the cuttings in the morning when the stems are most hydrated. Cut each stem immediately below a leaf to about 3 inches (7.5 cm) long. Remove leaves from the lower half of the stem and place the cuttings in pots of well-drained potting soil or a mixture of 3 parts perlite and 1 part peat moss. Several stems can be placed in each pot. Water the pots thoroughly and keep them at room temperature near a cool, yet brightly lit window. If the cuttings are very soft and start to wilt, place a plastic bag over the pot, holding it above the foliage by wire hoops, to increase the humidity. Salvia cuttings can make roots in a few weeks if conditions are optimum. Rooted cuttings can then be separated and potted in early spring to grow on and be ready for planting out at the appropriate time.

To overwinter tender salvias, place several cuttings in a pot and keep at room temperature near a window. Cover the pot with a plastic bag to increase the humidity; a wire hoop will keep the bag off the leaves.

Another way to overwinter tender salvias is by potting up the root ball. To do this, dig plants in the fall before a severe freeze. Cut the plants back hard and pot in appropriately sized containers with a well-draining soil mix. Water well. Store the potted specimens in a garage or basement where cool temperatures will not encourage new growth, and where the plants are protected from freezing temperatures. Water as needed through winter, not letting the soil become bone dry, yet allowing the soil to dry some between waterings. In spring, move the pots outside on days that are not too cold or windy, but bring them back inside during the nights. The tender new growth is very susceptible to frost. This process will harden the plants off before they are planted out for the season.

Often not all of the plant needs to be dug and saved. Many salvias increase at the base, in which case all that needs to be potted up is a piece from outside of the clump. Be sure the piece has roots attached to it. *Salvia leucantha* (Mexican bush sage) and *S. elegans* are two such plants where you may not need to pot up the entire root ball.

WHERE TO BUY

Most of the nurseries listed here have good display gardens worth visiting as well as informative websites. Because the business of being a plant nursery is unpredictable at best, call or visit websites prior to planning any visits to confirm open hours and locations.

AUSTRALIA

Unlimited Perennials
369 Boomerang Drive
Lavington, NSW 2641
www.salviaspecialist.com

UNITED KINGDOM

Ashwood Nurseries
Ashwood Lower Lane
Ashwood
Kingswinford
West Midlands
England DY6 0AE
www.ashwoodnurseries.com

Birchwood Plants
Gardener's Lane
Romsey
Hampshire
England S051 6AD
www.birchwoodplants.co.uk

Chiltern Seeds
The AC Bortree Stile
Ulverston
England LA12 7PB
www.chilternseeds.co.uk
Seeds.

Claire Austin Hardy Plants
White Hopton Farm
Wern Lane
Sarn
Newtown
England SY16 4EN
www.claireaustin-hardyplants.co.uk

Dyson's Nurseries at Great Comp
Great Comp Garden
Comp Lane
Platt
Sevenoaks
Kent
England TN15 8QS
www.greatcompgarden.co.uk
Specialist salvias catalog available.

Mr. Fothergill's
Kentford
Suffolk
England CB8 7QB
www.mr-fothergills.co.uk
Seeds.

Pennycross Plants
Earith Road, Colne
Huntingdon
Cambridgeshire
England PE28 3NL
www.pennycrossplants.co.uk

Phoenix Perennial Plants
Paice Lane, Medstead
Alton
Hampshire
England GU34 5PR
www.phoenixperennialplants.co.uk

Thompson and Morgan
Poplar Lane
Ipswich
Suffolk
England IP8 3BU
www.thompson-morgan.com
Mail-order seeds.

Unwins Seeds
Alconbury Hill
Huntingdon
England PE28 4HY
www.unwins.co.uk
Seeds.

UNITED STATES

Annie's Annuals
740 Market Avenue
Richmond, California 94801
www.anniesannuals.com
Mail-order and retail; display gardens.

California Flora Nursery
2990 Somers Street
Fulton, California 95349
www.calfloranursery.com
Retail only; display gardens.

Digging Dog Nursery
31101 Middle Ridge Road
Albion, California 95410
www.diggingdog.com
Retail and mail-order; display gardens.

Emerisa Gardens
555 Irwin Lane
Santa Rosa, California 95401
www.emerisa.com
Seasonal retail only.

Flowers by the Sea
Elk, California 95432
www.fbts.com
Mail-order only.

High Country Gardens
P.O. Box 22398
Santa Fe, New Mexico 87502
www.highcountrygardens.com
Mail-order only.

Las Pilitas
3232 Las Pilitas Road
Santa Margarita, California 93453
Retail and mail-order; display gardens.

Las Pilitas
8331 Nelson Way
Escondido, California 92026
www.laspilitas.com
Retail and mail-order; display gardens.

Lazy S'S Farm Nursery
2360 Spotswood Trail
Barboursville, Virginia 22923
www.lazyssfarm.com
Mail-order only.

Morningsun Herb Farm
6137 Pleasants Valley Road
Vacaville, California 95688
www.morningsunherbfarm.com
Retail and mail-order; display gardens.

Plant Delights Nursery
9241 Sauls Road
Raleigh, North Carolina 27603
www.plantdelights.com
Retail and mail-order; display gardens.

Seedhunt
P.O. Box 96
Freedom, California 95019
www.seedhunt.com
Mail-order seeds.

Theodore Payne Foundation
10459 Tuxford Street
Sun Valley, California 91352
www.theodorepayne.org
Retail; seeds; display gardens.

World of Salvias
2119 US 220 Alternate South
Candor, North Carolina 27229
www.worldofsalvias.com
Mail-order only.

WHERE TO SEE

Royal Tasmanian Botanical Gardens
Queens Domain
Hobart TAS 7000
www.rtbg.tas.gov.au

The Hardy Plant Society
15 Basepoint Business Centre
Crab Apple Way
Evesham
England WR11 1GP
www.hardy-plant.org.uk

National Collection of Species Salvias
Mr. and Mrs. J. Pink
2 Hillside Cottages
Trampers Lane
North Boarhunt
Fareham
Hampshire
England PO17 6DA
+044 (0) 1329 832786

National Collection of Tender Salvias
Nigel Hewish
Kingston Maurward Gardens
Kingston Maurward
Dorchester
England DT2 8PY
www.kmc.ac.uk/gardens

**Cabrillo College Environmental
Horticulture Center & Botanic Gardens**
6500 Soquel Drive
Aptos, California 95003
www.cabrillo.edu
*Primarily an educational display garden,
Cabrillo College Environmental Horticulture department does host an annual plant
sale. Has the largest institutional collection
of salvias in North America.*

Denver Botanic Gardens
1007 York Street
Denver, Colorado 80206
www.botanicgardens.org
*Primarily an educational display garden,
Denver Botanic Gardens has limited plants
for sale at shop and annual plant sales.*

Huntington Botanical Gardens
1151 Oxford Road
San Marino, California 91108
www.huntington.org

**Los Angeles County Arboretum
and Botanic Garden**
301 North Baldwin Avenue
Arcadia, California 91007
www.arboretum.org

Lurie Garden
Millenium Park
201 East Randolph Street
Chicago, IL 60602
www.cityofchicago.org/city/en/depts/
dca/supp_info/millennium_park_-
luriegarden.html

Rancho Santa Ana Botanic Garden
1500 North College Avenue
Claremont, California 91711
www.rsabg.org
*Garden dedicated to California
native plants.*

Sacramento Historic City Cemetery
1000 Broadway
Sacramento, California 95818
www.oldcitycemetery.com
*Home to three public gardens including
the Hamilton Square Perennial Garden
and Sacramento Chapter of the California
Native Plant Society's Native Plant
Demonstration Garden, both of which
feature many salvias.*

**San Francisco Botanical Garden at
Strybing Arboretum**
1199 9th Avenue
San Francisco, California 94122
www.sfbotanicalgarden.org
*Primarily an educational public display
garden. Has limited plants for sale at shop
and annual plant sales.*

Tilden Regional Park
Regional Parks Botanic Garden
Wildcat Canyon Road
Berkeley, California 94605
www.ebparks.org/parks/tilden/
botanic_garden

**University of California Botanical
Garden at Berkeley**
200 Centennial Drive
Berkeley, California 94720
botanicalgarden.berkeley.edu
*Primarily an educational public display
garden. Has limited plants for sale at shop
and annual plant sales.*

U.S. National Arboretum
3501 New York Avenue, NE
Washington, DC 20002
www.usna.usda.gov
*The National Herb Garden features 60 Sal-
via species and cultivars in autumn.*

Wave Hill
675 West 252nd Street
Bronx, New York 10471
www.wavehill.org

**WPA Rock Garden at
William Land Park**
3800 Land Park Drive
Sacramento, California 95822
www.cityofsacramento.org/
parksandrecreation/parks/sites/
land_photo.htm

FOR MORE INFORMATION

BOOKS

Armitage, Allan M. 2000. *Armitage's Garden Perennials: A Color Encyclopedia*. Portland, Oregon: Timber Press.

Armitage, Allan M. 2001. *Manual of Annuals, Biennials, and Half-Hardy Perennials*. Portland, Oregon: Timber Press.

Bailey, L. H. 1917. *The Standard Cyclopedia of Horticulture*. Vol. S–Z. New York: MacMillan.

Clausen, Ruth Rogers, and Nicolas H. Ekstrom. 1989. *Perennials for American Gardens*. New York: Random House.

Clebsch, Betsy. 2003. *The New Book of Salvias: Sages for Every Garden*. Portland, Oregon: Timber Press.

Hickman, James C. 1993. *The Jepson Manual: Higher Plants of California*. Berkeley and Los Angeles: University of California Press.

Jelitto, Leo, and William Schacht. 1950. *Hardy Herbaceous Perennials*. Vol. II, L–Z. Portland, Oregon: Timber Press.

Norris, Kathleen Brenzel, editor. 2001. *Sunset Western Garden Book*. Menlo Park, California: Sunset Publishing.

Perry, Bob. 2010. *Landscape Plants for California Gardens: An Illustrated Reference of Plants for California Landscapes*. Claremont, California: Land Design Publishing.

Phillips, Roger, and Nicky Foy. 1990. *The Random House Book of Herbs*. New York: Random House.

Phillips, Roger, and Martyn Rix. 1990. *The Random House Book of Perennials*. Vol. 2, *Late Perennials*. New York: Random House.

Smith, M. Nevin. 2006. *Native Treasures: Gardening with the Plants of California*. Berkeley and Los Angeles: University of California Press.

Sutton, John. 1999. *The Gardener's Guide to Growing Salvias*. Portland, Oregon: Timber Press.

Thomas, Graham Stuart. 1976. *Perennial Garden Plants: or The Modern Florilegium*. London: J. M. Dent in association with the Royal Horticultural Society.

WEBSITES

Robin's Salvias: www.robinssalvias.com. Created by British salvia enthusiast Robin Middleton, this is one man's website about all things related to the enjoyment and study of salvias.

Salvias of Argentina: www.salvias.com.ar. Managed by Argentinian salvia expert Rolando Uria of the University of Buenos Aires, Argentina. Site is in Spanish and has wonderful photos and comprehensive salvia information.

ORGANIZATIONS

Salvia Research Network: http://128.104.26.120/salvia/index.html. An international group focusing on taxonomy of salvias.

Salvia Study Group of Victoria: www.salvias.org.au. A branch of the Herb Society of Victoria devoted to the study and enjoyment of salvias in Australia.

HARDINESS ZONE TEMPERATURES

USDA ZONES & CORRESPONDING TEMPERATURES

Temp °F			Zone	Temp °C		
−60	to	−55	1a	−51	to	−48
−55	to	−50	1b	−48	to	−46
−50	to	−45	2a	−46	to	−43
−45	to	−40	2b	−43	to	−40
−40	to	−35	3a	−40	to	−37
−35	to	−30	3b	−37	to	−34
−30	to	−25	4a	−34	to	−32
−25	to	−20	4b	−32	to	−29
−20	to	−15	5a	−29	to	−26
−15	to	−10	5b	−26	to	−23
−10	to	−5	6a	−23	to	−21
−5	to	0	6b	−21	to	−18
0	to	5	7a	−18	to	−15
5	to	10	7b	−15	to	−12
10	to	15	8a	−12	to	−9
15	to	20	8b	−9	to	−7
20	to	25	9a	−7	to	−4
25	to	30	9b	−4	to	−1
30	to	35	10a	−1	to	2
35	to	40	10b	2	to	4
40	to	45	11a	4	to	7
45	to	50	11b	7	to	10
50	to	55	12a	10	to	13
55	to	60	12b	13	to	16
60	to	65	13a	16	to	18
65	to	70	13b	18	to	21

FIND HARDINESS MAPS ON THE INTERNET.
United States *http://www.usna.usda.gov/Hardzone/ushzmap.html*
Canada *http://www.planthardiness.gc.ca/* or *http://atlas.nrcan.gc.ca/site/ english/maps/environment/forest/forestcanada/planthardi*
Europe *http://www.gardenweb.com/zones/europe/* or *http://www.uk. gardenweb.com/forums/zones/hze.html*

ACKNOWLEDGMENTS

Writing a book is not a lone endeavor. Many people have been very supportive and helpful through this process. The local plant community in Chico was great: Chris and Courtney of Magnolia Gift and Garden located plants for me and allowed me freedom to rearrange plants in their nursery to photograph; the Flower Floozies at the Plant Barn always cheered me on; Christy Santos allowed me to photograph her colorful and artfully planted garden; and homeowners said yes when I knocked on their door asking permission to take photos.

I was extremely fortunate to have several great collections of salvias within a day's drive. Kermit and Vikki of Flowers by the Sea were gracious in allowing me to wander for hours studying plants and taking photos. Ernie Wasson introduced me to the large salvia collection at Cabrillo College, where I spent many hours. And a huge thank you to Sandi Martin, whose garden is beautiful and contains so many salvias positioned in a variety of settings; Sandi was generous in sharing not only her garden but also her hands-on experience in growing a diversity of salvias.

Salvias are diverse as are the climates in which they are grown, so I was appreciative for the contributions by Panayoti Kelaidis of the Denver Botanic Gardens, Richard Dufresne in North Carolina, Lili Singer of the Theodore Payne Foundation, and Robin Middleton in the United Kingdom.

Also a big thank you to my sister Lucy for her hearty encouragement; to Joan Walters who meticulously edited, helping me clean-up the writing; and to Jennifer Jewell who shared her experienced eye in assisting me with photo selection along with reading the manuscript and giving feedback throughout the lengthy process.

And to my Dad whose encouragement to accept this challenge tipped any doubt I harbored in the last conversation I had with him.

PHOTO CREDITS

Photographs are by the author except for the following:

COVER: (front & spine) iStockphoto/zorani; (back top left) iStockphoto/aimintang; (back bottom) iStockphoto/piyathep.

DAVE BEVAN/GAP, page 109 right.

WILLIAM DYSON, pages 90 left and 116 left.

JENNIFER JEWELL, pages 30 bottom, 42 bottom, 68 left, 89, 116 right, 123, 129, 191, and 218.

PANAYOTI KELAIDIS, page 66 bottom.

ISTOCKPHOTO/AIMINTANG, pages 2–3.

ISTOCKPHOTO/AYIMAGES, pages 4–5.

ISTOCKPHOTO/FOTOLINCHEN, pages 188–189.

ISTOCKPHOTO/PIYATHEP, pages 48–49.

ISTOCKPHOTO/ZORANI, pages 10–11 and 54–55.

INDEX

ABOUT THE AUTHOR

Owner of Canyon Creek Nursery and Design in interior Northern California, **JOHN WHITTLESEY** is a nurseryman, garden designer, landscape contractor, and avid amateur photographer. As a specialty grower and a designer, he enjoys interesting plants and creating attractive, water-conserving gardens that provide habitat for people and wildlife. Salvias have long been among his favorites and, due to his early interest in this plant group, the Canyon Creek Nursery catalog had one of the first extensive offerings of salvias in the country. Today John continues to incorporate salvias generously into his gardens, although he no longer operates a mail-order nursery. He is a graduate of the California School of Garden Design. A retrospective of his career was profiled in the spring 2011 issue of *Pacific Horticulture*.

Front cover: 'Caradonna'
Spine: 'Amethyst'
Title page: *Salvia leucantha*
Contents page: *Salvia viridis*

The Haseltine Building   6a Lonsdale Road
133 S.W. Second Avenue, Suite 450 London NW6 6RD
Portland, Oregon 97204-3527

For details on other Timber Press books and to
sign up for our newsletters, please visit our websites,
timberpress.com and timberpress.co.uk.

Library of Congress Cataloging-in-Publication Data
Whittlesey, John, 1953-
  The plant lover's guide to salvias/John Whittlesey. —First edition.
    pages cm
  Other title: Salvias
  Includes index.
  ISBN 978-1-60469-419-2
  1. Salvia. 2. Gardening. I. Title. II. Title: Salvias.
  SB413.S22W48 2014
  635—dc23   2013034038

A catalog record for this book is also available from the British Library.

Book and cover design by Laken Wright
Layout and composition by Ben Patterson
Printed in China

THE **PLANT LOVER'S GUIDE** TO
DAHLIAS
ANDY VERNON

THE **PLANT LOVER'S GUIDE** TO
SEDUMS
BRENT HORVATH

THE **PLANT LOVER'S GUIDE** TO
SNOWDROPS
NAOMI SLADE